Fairy Boys

Daniel Tawse

Fairy Boys by Daniel Tawse was first published in 2019
by Amazon Kindle Direct Publishing
www.kdp.amazon.com

PB ISBN 978-1-9161116-0-8

eBook © May 2019 ISBN 978-1-9161116-1-5

For my family.

One.

The summer holidays had gone on for far too long.

It had been a week. *Yep*. A whole week spent on my own. Seven days of actually missing school. One hundred and sixty-eight hours of staring out of my bedroom window at the field behind the houses, where the other boys hung out, their cheekbones glistening in the heat. I watched them as they mucked about topless in the hot sun, flexing to girls who, if they were lucky, buried their noses into soft cotton t-shirts on the sidelines.

Their summer was about friendship, and constant laughter, and making memories that would stay with them until the fine hairs around their temples turned coarse and white.

And mine was about me, Star Stephenson, going quietly insane.

To enjoy a summer on our estate, you had to be funny or good-looking. It was really as simple as that. You had to be able to fire one-liners faster than the speed of light, before your opponent even had time to think. Or you had to be muscly, with a thick neck and a straight collarbone.

I had none of this. I was cut from a different cloth; one that snagged and curved and gathered in awkward places, like ruched curtains. It was no wonder I didn't fit in—our estate was no place for ruched curtains. Our estate was no place for anything remotely vibrant, actually. Each house, identical to the next, was penned into a shoebox-sized plot, surrounded by shallow, yet-to-be-painted metal fences. The gardens were narrow, the white, plastic window frames were narrower, and the roofs were flatter than a witch's boob.

If it were up to me, I would live on the other side of the field behind the houses, in the newly built flats, where blue lights cast by giant flat-screen televisions flashed through perfect windows every night. I would have neighbours and friends. I would have laughter and memories. I would be able to bury my nose into a soft cotton t-shirt and look up from it to see someone smiling back at me.

And I knew exactly how it would feel, and I knew exactly how it would smell—clean, like mint shower gel or talcum powder or Lynx Africa body spray.

But summers like that didn't happen to boys like me.

What more was there to say? I just needed the holidays to be over. That was all. The prospect of sitting in my bedroom for the foreseeable future filled me with dread. And though school was hell, it was surely better than purgatory.

'What a *Shiloh Pitt* this is,' came a voice from below. I looked down beyond the back fence to see a pair of huge, dark eyes staring at me. 'You've got to be joking—if you're going to tell me you've spent another day inside, Star Stephenson,' the voice said, 'I think I'm going to flip. You've got twenty seconds.' I watched the eyes disappear and a small shape move quickly along the back fences.

Immediately I leapt from my seat by the window and ran onto the landing. I swung a leg over the banister and slid down, skidding across the carpet when I hit the ground.

She stood on the top step looking sun-flushed—her curly hair twisted into two buns, one on each side of her head. 'Nineteen and a half—twenty! There he is,' she said, smiling with thick teeth that looked huge in such a tiny head, her big eyes still staring. She had ice cream gathered around the edges of her mouth, like a five-year-old. 'Thought I'd grab one of these from Giovanni's van. Want some?'

I shook my head.

'Suit yourself.'

Her name was Naseera Connolly—or Naz, as the others called her—and she lived in the flat above Connolly's Chippy, which meant she smelt like deep-fried vinegar. I didn't mind at all—she was the only person who ever spoke to me.

'What did you mean when you said *Shiloh Pitt*?' I said.

'It's the new thing,' she said, licking melted ice cream off her hand. 'Brad Pitt and Angelina Jolie named their kid Shiloh Pitt, but if you swap the beginnings of each word around, it sort of sounds like pile of sh—'

'Right. Okay—I get it.'

'Good, isn't it?'

I shrugged. 'Sure. Poor kid.'

'Yeah, well, speaking of that,' she said, 'you shouldn't stay inside on a day like today.' I pretended not to hear her. 'I know why you're doing it—I can read you like a book, Star Stephenson. You shouldn't let those lads bother you. They're idiots. You're different—one of a kind. You should be proud of that.'

I flicked my eyes towards her, too embarrassed to disagree, but secretly wishing to myself that one day I would be just like the other boys—sun-tanned and handsome and funny, surrounded by so many friends I couldn't name them all. That's what summer was supposed to look like. Not this.

'Suit yourself, again,' she said.

A woman appeared at the end of the street. 'Naseera Connolly!' she shouted.

The sound of car horns smashed into my head as the woman stepped out onto the road without looking.

Naseera dropped her cone on the step. It landed with a splat—pointy end up, splashing ice cream onto one side of my leg.

'It's me mam,' she said.

All of the kids on the estate were scared of mean old Mrs Connolly, and with good reason. She was a solid, round woman who could move surprisingly quickly for someone of her shape. She was at the front gate before we had time to think.

'I took the money for the ice cream from the old cow's purse,' said Naseera. 'It was only a fiver. Oh, bloody hell. She's going to kill me. They'll find me body buried under the chippy wrapped in yesterday's newspaper. Come on.' She grabbed my hand and pulled me into the house.

She ran through the kitchen and pulled the back door open. We ripped through layers of bedding strung from a washing line that zigzagged across the yard. 'You're going to have to give me a leg up,' she said when we reached the back fence.

I interlocked my fingers and grabbed one of her small trainers. She gripped the top of the fence and, with a shove, curled over it and landed in the thicket on the other side.

Without thinking, I hurled myself over, landing on my feet just beyond the bush.

Then we ran as fast as we could. Long blades of overgrown grass whipped my bare legs as we leapt over dried-out puddles of mud and made our way around the edge of a rowdy game of five-a-side football.

'Here, Star! You lanky prick,' shouted one of the boys. 'You run like a proper lass.'

Both teams stopped what they were doing and began to laugh.

'Here comes the biggest fairy in Newcastle,' shouted another.

I had foolishly believed that being stuck inside all summer was as bad as things were going to get. I was so very wrong. Standing in an open field with an entire group of boys laughing their heads off at me was a brand new low. I had never felt more aware of myself; my girly legs, my skinny arms.

In a moment of blind panic, I turned around and stuck two fingers up at them.

Immediately, the match was over. Sun-blushed boys with perfectly blended hairdos turned into careless thugs with angry faces and began to sprint towards me.

'Think you're brave 'cos you've got your little mate with you, half-gadge?' yelled one of them.

I hated that name. Out of all the horrible things they called me, that was the worst. Half-gadge. I took it to mean half-boy, half-girl—like I was a mix of both, not wholly either. Not complete—not a real person with real feelings. It cut me. And I let them call me it because in a strange way I identified with it. I wasn't like the other boys, and I wasn't like the girls. I was somewhere in the middle, halfway between being something and being nothing. Not funny enough, not good-looking enough, nowhere near masculine enough—I probably felt it more than they could see it.

I wanted to stop. I wanted to stand rooted to the spot and let them all come for me. But I wasn't brave.

So I ran.

I had fled from a hiding enough times to know every alleyway, back lane and short cut on the estate. I had my wits about me. Sometimes I felt like that was all I had.

My feet pounded the hard ground as I twisted around sharp corners and jumped fences. I ran to the end of the Scotswood Road, over the motorway, and down towards the quayside, making a sharp turn under a railway bridge when I reached the bank.

I pressed my back against a cold wall, closing my eyes as

if this would make me invisible.

A train galloped past, each new carriage ricocheting off the old tracks like a heartbeat. *One, two*. It pierced through my chest, throwing me off rhythm. *One, two*. Were they about to get me? *One, two*. I wanted to scream through the noise, but at the same time I wanted to hide in it.

Oh Lord, if you're listening, it's me—Star. It's been a while. Please, please, please make a giant hole open up in the ground so I can fall through it and never be seen again. Failing that, the usual stuff will do—a swarm of locusts, a pox on their houses. You know the drill. If you get me out of this one, I promise I'll go back to Sunday school. Please, I'm desperate. Amen.

A hand burst through the noise, grabbing the side of my shirt. 'What the hell were you thinking?' My eyes clicked open. It was Naseera. 'Have you got a death wish?' she said.

The train made its final round overhead. *One, two*—the loudest of them all. An echo rang off her last word. *Wish. Wish. Wish*. 'You don't stick your fingers up at boys like that,' she said. 'Ignore them, yes, pretend they don't exist, sure—but sticking your fingers up? You're lucky to be alive, man.'

I allowed my heartbeat to dull in my ears as I caught my breath. I tried to focus on her, on her words. But all I could think about was the name they had called me. It still twisted inside of my stomach. I wished I had thought of something just as clever to say back. I was such a bloody coward. Running only made things ten times worse.

I must have been someone terrible in a past life; Jack the Ripper, maybe, or Margaret Thatcher. And when they were handing out next-lives, they must have had a real struggle in deciding whether I should be the most ridiculed boy in all of Newcastle, or a dung beetle.

I could see it now; God sitting on a golden throne, swathed in white robes, with Jesus on one side and Oprah Winfrey on the other. He would say: *what should we do with this one? He murdered a handful of prostitutes and got away with it.* Or: *this one nicked everyone's milk and supported capital punishment. I know just what to do with her ...*

Whichever it was, in the end, they made the right decision. Living this life was the worst penance a soul could ask for; even worse than spending an eternity rolling big lumps of crap around.

'I'm going to say it again, Star,' Naseera began, 'this time really slowly. You-have-to-ig-nore-them. That's it. Don't hide in your bedroom. Don't stick your fingers up at them. Just ignore them like they don't matter.'

It was easy for her to say. They never bothered her. She looked like she was supposed to look. Her voice and face and arms and legs all matched; all fitted.

And, the truth was, I didn't want to ignore them. I wanted to be a popular boy, with high cheekbones and caramel skin and flushed cheeks and shaved hair on the sides. I wanted to hang out on the backfield and wear brand new Nike Air Max 95s. I wanted everything they had and nothing I had.

Naseera just didn't understand.

I turned around to walk away from her.

'Where are you going?' she asked.

I didn't answer. Just kept walking. She would get the hint.

'Hello!' she shouted, her voice echoing under the bridge, 'Star, where are you going?'

I didn't look back. What was the point? They had won. They always won.

'Fine,' she shouted. 'Get lost, then.'

I wanted to be angry. I wanted to be brave. I wanted to be able to stick up for myself. Real boys respected that. I had seen it happen before; smaller kids squaring up to bigger ones, making them back down. That was the only way to survive around here. I should have said something back to them. Letting them get to me only made them worse.

I was such an idiot.

I walked until the sky turned darker and the streetlights came on. Without the sun, the night air was cold, backed by a wind that ran up the streets and scraped along the back fences like sticks. Sirens and raised voices and smashing windows stabbed into the darkness, exploding on street corners and alleyways. Our estate wasn't a place to be wandering around alone at night, no matter who you were.

The orange light of a streetlamp shone onto our house. I didn't want to go in. Crossing the threshold meant I was officially on my own. I looked up at the small square windows and flat roof. I didn't see a home at all; didn't see a place full of good memories. It was just a shoebox full of broken things, like the ones Mam used to keep under her bed.

I turned my key in the lock and pushed the front door away from its white, plastic frame.

The house was lit by one table lamp. *Match of the Day* was on the television. The place smelt like cigarette smoke and stale fabric softener. Dad was asleep on the sofa, a half-eaten plate of chips and curry sauce on the floor next to him. I bent down and grabbed one. I was starving.

'Where have you been?' asked a voice.

I didn't answer.

'Star?' he said. He took in a heavy breath and opened one eye. 'You can't just go wandering off on your own without telling anyone where you are.'

I hadn't meant to wander for so long. I hadn't planned to do that. It just happened. I needed some time to think. I wanted to say sorry, but my words tangled into a giant knot in my throat, like they always did when I tried to speak to him.

'Look,' he continued, sitting up. 'I want to talk to you. I know how hard it is being thirteen. Believe it or not, I was thirteen once—'

'Fourteen,' I said.

'What?'

'I'm fourteen,' I said, 'and a half.'

'Right—are you sure?'

I nodded.

'Well, okay, what I'm trying to say is, whatever it is that's bothering you, it'll pass. Just get on with things and one day it won't matter as much.'

It'll pass.

Just get on with things.

Why did nobody understand—couldn't he see me? The way I felt wouldn't just pass; being a fairy wouldn't just pass; being a friendless half-gadge wouldn't just pass. Those things were for life. I wasn't going through some teenage phase. It had nothing to do with being fourteen and a half, actually—there was far more to it than that. I was full of things I couldn't explain, full of anger and bits that didn't fit.

I was the only person I knew who was like me. Being fourteen and a half was the least of my problems.

'It won't,' I said.

I walked out of the room and up the stairs to my bedroom, flopping onto the bed when I got there.

I want to change, I thought, squeezing my head. *I need to change.*

Out of my window, over the field, I could see into living rooms. Families gathered on sofas, or around small tables, illuminated by the flashing blue lights of flat-screen televisions. They held each other; they laughed together; they argued over who was holding the remote.

The pain in my chest grew too quickly. I felt like my heart had been replaced with a chunk of ice, and it was trying to push through my rubbery tubes—stretching them in ways they weren't made to be stretched; tearing them as it moved slowly and heavily down towards my stomach.

Every part of me ached to be like everybody else; to have the things they had. Every part of me ached to be accepted; to have friends and a family.

I buried my face into my pillow, squeezing my eyes tightly closed and willing the tears to go away. I knew proper boys didn't cry.

But heat seared my forehead, and soon my cheekbones were wet. I couldn't stop them. The frustration I felt buzzed in the tips of my fingers, stung in my gums, raced up and down the sides of my body like electricity. I wanted to climb out of it; climb out of myself—unzip myself like a sleeping bag and leave this person, whoever he was, behind.

I yelped into the stuffing, unable to control the hurt that rose from somewhere way down inside of me; somewhere I thought it was buried. My belly vibrated and my lips cracked, but I couldn't stop.

I cried until there was nothing left—until I was completely drained.

Soon I was still, following a crack in the ceiling from the light fitting to the window and back again, the voice inside my head, my only true voice, speaking the same words over and over again.

I need to change.

I need to change.

I need to change.

Baby.

She spoke in her real voice; her strong voice, not the whisper that existed only my head.

Wake up, baby.

I could feel the dip in the mattress at the end of my bed, weighed down by her body. My feet rolled towards her.

What's wrong?

I could smell her clean hair, my favourite smell. I wanted to open my eyes. I wanted to see her smiling mouth again.

But I had been here before, maybe a hundred times. I knew if I opened my eyes she would go. If I moved towards her she would run away. She was air; she was water; she was sand—I couldn't hold her in my hands. I couldn't keep any part of her with me. She was free to come and go as she pleased.

Star, she whispered.

'Don't go,' I said. My eyelids started to loosen. 'Stay here with me.'

It doesn't work like that, baby, she whispered.

'Please.'

My eyelashes fluttered on my cheeks. I couldn't stop them. My eyes cracked open slowly.

I was alone. She had never been there. She would never be there.

And I so needed her.

Two.

Dad opened the bedroom door. Quietly. He needn't have bothered. I wasn't asleep. I had watched the sun rise over the rooftops, shining light on a new day.

The estate looked calm after another night of raised voices and smashing glass; covered in mist that weaved in and around the grey and the brown. I knew, however, that by the time the sun had moved past the houses along the top road, things would change. And I was right. The noises—the teasing, the flirting, the sniggering—rattled my bedroom window on cue, as boys and girls carried on with their summer, trying to pretend they were separate when all they really wanted to be was together. That's all I wanted too. But boys were boys and girls were girls. Each side had very specific entry requirements, and I was too inconsistent to fit in either. Which left me somewhere in between the two, lost in no-friends land.

'Are you awake?' he asked. His voice was brittle. I hadn't heard it like that for a while.

I sat forward and plumped the pillow behind me. It was wet. My morning-mouth tasted sour and dry, and my head felt heavier than usual. Another sleepless night had left me frayed around the edges, like the curtains that hung by the window.

'Can we talk?' Dad said. He took a seat at the end of the bed. In the harsh light of morning he looked proper old, with deep, sad shadows all over his face. 'There's someone here to see you,' he continued. My forehead burned when I thought of Naseera, standing at the bottom of the stairs. I owed her an apology. 'She arrived early this morning. I didn't ask her to. Anyway, she's here and she wants to have a word with you—Shuna.'

The door scraped further against the carpet and a woman appeared behind it. She was tall, with dark, curly hair, cut up to her ears so it fanned out like the rim of a hat.

'This is my sister, Shuna,' Dad said.

'Hello, Star,' said the woman. Her voice was deep and coarse; it boomed off the bedroom walls, filling the space with noise. 'Absolute pleasure—heard so much about you.'

She sort of looked like Dad, but older, with darker, blacker eyes that twinkled when she smiled. She wore a blue dress, cut above the knee. It was really creased and covered in a red cherry pattern. Odd socks flopped over her shins, above scuffed brown boots. Silver bracelets and charms covered her wrists. She jangled towards the bed and brought with her the smell of outside—of wind and grass and smoke. I liked that smell.

'Shuna wants to ask you something,' said Dad.

'Yes,' said Shuna. 'I wondered if you'd like to come and spend the summer with me?'

'Shuna lives by the sea,' said Dad, quickly. He held out a postcard. It was a picture of a beach. On the sea floated three tiny boats with tall masts, surrounded by water that was as blue as washing-up liquid. I squinted my tired eyes to get a better look at it. Across the top was written: *Greetings From Beadnell Bay.* 'I think it might do us both good to get out of Newcastle.'

I felt the edges of my mouth curl upwards. I couldn't stop them. That was exactly what I wanted. Anywhere was better than here.

'You look brighter already,' said Shuna. She smiled and her eyes disappeared into folds of shiny skin. 'That settles it. We'll take a train tomorrow.'

Dad stood from the end of the bed, a little bit straighter, before walking out of the room with Shuna and pressing the door closed.

Silence rang off the damp-stained walls as I sat completely still, unsure of what to do next. I followed a crack in the wallpaper right down to the radiator, where it rippled and curled away from the wall to expose whatever had been there before: some green and brown floral pattern by the looks of it.

I was going somewhere—getting out of Newcastle. I was going to have a proper summer, with beach towels and sun cream and fish and chips. Just like those kids who went on family holidays to Majorca or Benidorm.

A flame ignited in my stomach, clicking on like a lighter.

I jumped up from the bed and pulled out my backpack from under it. I reached in and grabbed the schoolbooks, pens and empty crisp packets that sat crumpled at the bottom and threw them to one side. Then I tied my long hair up on top of my head, and laid all of my best clothes out on the bed—the denim shorts; an Adidas t-shirt; two vintage American baseball shirts that I'd begged Dad to buy me from town, back when he used to go out; my high-top Converse and a rogue item—a white string vest that I had secretly cut so it hung just above my belly button. I didn't think I would wear it, but I had room, so I packed it.

I placed all of them, along with my toothbrush, inside the bag and pulled the drawstring. I was packed. That was easy.

I walked over to the window and looked at the field. The boys were performing their usual ritual of whipping girls with their t-shirts, making sure the muscles on their upper arms were tensed when they did it. My eyes grew dry watching them.

They all looked the same; moved the same; sounded the same. *How did they know how to do that?* It was like a handbook titled *How to be a Boy* had been posted into all of the houses on the estate, and the postman couldn't be bothered to navigate his way around the weeds and empty lager cans, so hadn't delivered my copy. I had missed the memo, and in the meantime I had missed out on making friends.

But no one in Beadnell Bay knew that. I had the opportunity to rewrite history. I could hang out on the beach with friends, real friends, not people who thought I was weird. In Beadnell Bay I wasn't weird; I was another holidaymaker, just like everybody else.

I closed the window to shut off the noise. I didn't need to hear it anymore. I was about to make my own memories. I didn't need to waste another second living in their summer. Mine was going to be twice as good. Anybody could hang out on the backfield; anybody could drink cider outside the chippy. But I was the only one who was going to spend five whole weeks away from it all.

The taxi pulled up against the kerb, growling like a shiny black beast. I watched it from my position on the top step, my knees drawn up to my chest. I found it strange to be leaving—to be going somewhere I had never been before. I had a feeling that the next time I saw the street it wouldn't look the same. I let that sting for a moment.

The morning was perfect. Weirdly. From the reaching weeds poking up through cracked paving stones to the tiny greenflies weaving around the lampposts and the gentle heating of the tarmac. Ironically, Newcastle had never looked more like somewhere I could call home.

My belly filled with a hundred butterflies, all beating their bodies against my rib cage.

Ever since I had got out of bed that morning, a voice inside my head had been telling me to get back in it; to hide under the duvet and wait for the holidays to pass. That same voice told me I was making a huge mistake; the kids in Beadnell would be just like the boys at home.

'Taxi for number six?' asked the man.

'That's right,' said Shuna, appearing in the doorway.

Dad appeared behind her. He looked different—less crooked. He wore long smart trousers and a shirt, buttoned up.

It had been a long time since I had seen him look so presentable.

He brushed past me, and the smell of aftershave and Fox's mints filled my nostrils.

'We're going to have a lovely time,' said Shuna as I joined them on the back seat.

The driver closed the door, 'Central, was it?' he asked.

'Please, mate,' said Dad.

The car growled louder and moved to the end of the street, turning left and out of the estate. I watched our house get even smaller and then disappear behind a block of flats.

It was gone.

Central Station was huge, with loads of different bridges and staircases leading to hidden platforms. It was really old, too; the giant blocks that made up the entrance had turned grey and black. I imagined that once upon a time they were a golden colour. But colour couldn't exist in Newcastle; sooner or later everything turned grey and black.

We were to board the 12:30 to Aberdeen, though we were leaving the train at a place called Berwick-upon-Tweed.

'Tickets, please,' said the woman standing by the carriage entrance. Her scratched name badge read Kelly-Anne.

Shuna plucked three orange tickets from her purse—a purple beaded satin thing, crinkled and covered in tiny elephants.

'Thanks, flower,' said Kelly-Anne. She was very loud, with skin that was plump and crinkled like Shuna's purse, except it was bright orange instead of purple, and she had a double chin in the space where her neck was supposed to be that wobbled when she spoke. She punched a hole in the tickets and handed them back, smiling with teeth that were covered in coral-coloured lipstick. 'Here you go,' she said, already looking at the person behind.

'Thanks, pet,' said Dad, stepping onto the train.

Once we pulled away from the platform, it didn't take long before the graffiti-covered bricks, squashed houses, warehouses, cranes and bridges of Newcastle were far behind us, and we were flying through the countryside.

I had never seen anything like it. The further north we travelled, the bigger it became. Fields turned to mountains and trees turned to forests—the world was wilder in the north, rougher around the edges. The butterflies in my stomach changed into something far more substantial—maybe dragonflies or hummingbirds.

Beyond Morpeth, we met the sea. The train ran alongside it for miles as it stretched out forever, uninterrupted by anything. Though Newcastle seemed huge, it was nothing compared to the sea—nothing compared to this never-ending possibility that couldn't be disturbed by rooftops or bridges or blocks of flats.

When I stepped onto the platform at Berwick, the fresh air hit me like a bucket of water—cold, clean and sweet. I took giant gulps of it and allowed my lungs to stretch wider than they ever had before. I licked my lips and tasted salt. I was so obviously far away from the city, where the air stank of wheelie bins and petrol fumes.

We rode in the taxi with the windows down. The wind blew into my face, beating my cheeks awake. Dad sat beside me, his eyes closed and his thin lips spread in a smile. We hadn't done anything together in such a long time. I had spoken to him more in the past day than I had in ages. Somehow we were sharing an adventure again.

I felt strange. Excited, but an aware-excited. It was weird; I was really looking forward to getting away from Newcastle, but I sort of felt uneasy having Dad there. I wanted everything to be as uncomplicated as possible, but I felt like Dad found it hard to relax sometimes.

Maybe he would be different in Beadnell. Maybe things would be better. Looking at him just then, I believed they could be.

The car pulled into the village and stopped by a white-painted cottage that backed onto a field. I thought cottages had to be quaint, with thatched roofs and rose bushes outside. This one was a total rebel—all square blocks and sharp edges, with wide glass windows and a painted-blue slate roof. The garden was full of fluorescent rocks and weird animal statues.

I pushed open the gate with my foot and made my way up the garden path, passing a giraffe and heading towards a glass porch full of jars filled with pink jam and wasps. Above the door hung a cluster of brightly painted stones with holes drilled through their middles. They were tied together with blue rope.

Shuna ferreted in her bag for a set of keys. 'They're in here somewhere,' she said, turning it upside down and spilling its contents onto the step. She had a lot of stuff; more of the colourful stones, used tissues, receipts and old packets of nuts that had been crushed to sand all fell to the ground. 'Ah-ha!' she said, holding up a golden key.

She rubbed the hanging stones between her fingers as she crossed the threshold.

The cottage's rebellious streak continued inside. It was a festival of colours and houseplants and smells.

'Come in, come in,' said Shuna. 'Welcome home.' She fanned her long fingers and smiled widely.

'This is the furthest Star has been from Newcastle,' Dad said.

'Oh, my dear boy,' said Shuna. 'Then we must make sure your time here is glorious—Northumberland is an ancient kingdom, you know, full to the brim with fae folk—that's fairies to you city lot. Full of dunnies, hobthrushes and will-o'-the-wykes.' She leant in closer to me and held her hand to the side of her mouth before speaking again in more of a whisper. 'Always be brave enough to look for them.' She winked.

I liked Shuna. She was odd, but I sort of liked odd. I could tell she absolutely believed everything she said. I looked at Dad and wondered how two siblings could be so completely different.

In her own environment, Shuna really came to life. In my bedroom, she had been a novelty; an outbreak of colour and noise where there usually was none. But here, she was even more than that.

She began to sweep about the place, opening windows, causing things to jangle and clack, and lighting long twigs of incense so the place filled with sweet white smoke. 'Go through to the garden,' she said, throwing a pair of French doors open. 'I'll see what I can do for lunch.'

At the bottom of the garden there was a gate in the opening of a grey wall. Black moss grew between the old stones. Along the top of the wall, more brightly painted stones like the ones hanging by the door glowed purple and turquoise and red. Beyond, a sea of grass ran away to mountains of sand dunes covered in yellow hair that billowed in the wind. Dunes big enough to get lost in. Then came the great unknown—the blue forever.

Space like that had never existed to me before. The field behind the cottage must have been three times the size of the field on the estate. I felt tiny compared to it, like a goldfish that had been released into a pond. Fish like that grew abnormally large—they changed size to adapt to their habitat.

I took a deep, salty breath and wondered if I would do the same—if the bigness of the field and the sea would change me.

Later on, Shuna showed me to the bedroom that would be mine for the coming weeks. The place I was determined to spend as little time in as possible; the place where I was determined I would not hide away on my own.

It was very comfortable, with a big window right next to the bed that opened out onto the field, and coloured cushions all over the duvet. The walls were panelled with beige wood and covered with watercolour pictures of sailing boats. It was a world away from my room in Newcastle; everything looked clean and new.

'If there's anything you need at all,' Shuna began, 'just ask. I'll leave you to unpack. Your holiday will be magical here, Star. I'll make sure of it.'

Afterwards I lay down on the bed and watched the sky change from blue to orange and then to black. There were more stars in Beadnell than I had ever seen in Newcastle, like a fistful of salt had been thrown across the sky. The night was actually more than black and white; it was dust clouds of navy and silver and pink and a hundred other colours in between that I couldn't name.

Someone once told me that stars were special—proof that magic existed in the world. That's why it was my name.

Baby.

I suddenly remembered who had told me that. Her honey-soft voice whispered in my ear.

Goodnight, baby.

I could faintly see her tongue moving between her perfect teeth. I had tried so hard to stop seeing her like this; I had been told so many times to focus on what was real, but in this place she seemed realer than ever—the colours and the sea and the stars made her that way. I was glad she had followed me here.

For a blissful moment, I allowed myself to believe in her

again.

‘Goodnight, Mam,’ I whispered.

Three.

I woke to the smell of frying bacon seeping under my door as a church bell chimed somewhere, seven times.

The sky was already bright and filled with the sounds of cows and sheep and birds—sounds I never thought I would wake up to. It was a welcome change from the noises on the estate. I had heard enough of those to last a lifetime.

I yawned and stretched as tall as I could, the bones in my elbows and shoulders clicking awake.

Out in the garden, Dad sat at the table, reading a newspaper. 'Morning,' he said.

I took a seat opposite him. A pile of bacon sandwiches sat on a plate in the middle of the table. I reached forward and took one, biting into the soft, fresh bread and salty, crisp bacon. It tasted so good.

'Did you sleep well?'

I nodded as I chewed.

'Morning, Star,' said Shuna, emerging from the cottage in a wide-rimmed wicker hat and a long green kaftan, which didn't look too dissimilar to the curtains in my bedroom. 'Another glorious morning,' she continued, taking in a deep breath through triangular-shaped nostrils. 'The fae folk must be in a friendly mood. The wind is low and the sun is strong. Good day for the beach.'

I was excited to go to the beach. The beach would be where all of the action happened; Beadnell's equivalent to the field behind the houses on the estate. I would spend my summer there, sunbathing and swimming in the day and hanging out with friends at night.

'I've packed a hamper,' said Shuna, 'if you wouldn't mind helping me carry some deck chairs, Star, we'll be all set for the day.'

I reached for another sandwich. Things were getting off to a brilliant start.

After breakfast, we made our way across the field.

About halfway between the cottage and the dunes, a run-down caravan sat sunken into the ground. Parked beside it was an old Range Rover covered in dried mud. I hadn't noticed them the day before.

The remnants of a fire sat in front of the caravan. Black and orange embers, still warm and silver around the edges, glowed on the ground. They were surrounded by a circle of stones, and four foldaway chairs sat facing in different directions.

Although the fire hadn't long since burned down, there was nobody around to lay claim to it; the caravan door was closed, and net curtains covered the windows.

Dad grabbed my arm and hurried me past. He didn't even want to acknowledge that the caravan was there.

The lush grass grew far wilder as it met the sand dunes. Golden needles brushed my bare skin as I cut through, leaving tiny red marks all over me. By the time I got to the other side, I looked like I had contracted some sort of tropical disease. My skin itched and rose, but I didn't care. The view of the beach numbed every feeling I had—apart from joy.

It was the wind that told me I had cleared the dunes. It blew past my face and ran its fingers through my hair. Suddenly, like the flash of a camera, my world became light. Grey and brown were replaced with brilliant white, edged by yellow and green and blue. I couldn't open my eyes properly. The reflection of the sun on the sea meant the world was twice as bright—twice as good. Better than a postcard. I moved forward and the sand, soft as caster sugar, crawled between my toes and stuck there.

My summer was going to play out in paradise. In another world—a realer world, with wind and water and fire; a world that shrugged off the pretence of crammed-in bridges and pollution. A world that only had time for the stuff that mattered.

I wished the other boys on the estate could have seen me now—I wished they could have spent the day here to see what they were missing. Maybe they would be different. Maybe they would be kinder. Maybe under a light so bright, my flaws would be bleached-out, less obvious, and we could all just be friends.

'Tide is on its way in,' said Shuna, dropping her chair on the sand. 'If we set up too close, we'll only have to move later.'

Dad stood watching his sister struggle to hammer a broom handle into the sand with her shoe. The light of the sun made him look grey, like a stone column from Central Station. 'I don't know why it took me so long to come,' he said.

I didn't know, either. He had never mentioned Beadnell to me once, and we had spent some horrible summers together, sitting in dark rooms, while life happened somewhere else. A trip here would have changed everything.

I spread my towel out on the sand, flicking grains off the corners with my fingers. I didn't lie on it though. Not yet. I couldn't hold back any longer. I needed to know what sea water felt like.

The ground changed from powdery to dense and grooved as I walked towards the water. The wet sand was harder than concrete against my bare feet. Shells and seaweed and stones all sunbathed on the shore, waiting for the sea to grab them again so they could move on. I picked up a stone and clenched it in the palm of my hand. It was smooth, like skin. I hadn't expected it to be. I held it to my cheek.

The sea spread over the sand in layers, like sheets of glass, teasing it by moving forward smoothly, and then quickly rushing back, clawing at it and lifting it up, like an industrial digger. I thought the water would be blue, but it was so clear. I waded in, up to my knees, beige sand rising and swirling around my ankles with every new step I took.

A school of tiny grey fish darted past me. I didn't flinch. I felt realer out in the wild—calmer, and even a little bit braver.

I wondered how far I could go. I wondered what was out there. The possibilities were endless. The horizon stretched forever. I could have swum for as long as I wanted and never have reached it. I could have shouted as loudly as I liked and nobody over there would have heard me.

I splashed my arms and wet my hair and let the breeze give me goose bumps. I shivered and laughed and clapped my hand over my mouth as my shoulders rose up and down. I was free.

'Was that just gorgeous?' asked Shuna as I dripped back across the beach to my towel.

I lay down and tilted my head back to the sun. Warmth pressed over my face, down from my forehead, and around my eyes like gentle hands. Healing hands.

And time came to a stop. All the noises I carried around with me dulled to a whisper. Nothing else mattered but the sun, the sand, and the sound of waves smoothing against it.

'Yes,' I said.

We stayed on the beach all day, until the sun burned the sky orange and the sea came right up to the edge of my towel. It was a different place when the tide came in. Rougher. The grass on the dunes moved even faster, and the sea became choppy and grey. It was as if the beach had had enough of people for the day and was throwing everyone out.

We packed up our things and made our way through the dunes and across the field.

The caravan didn't look abandoned now; the door was

stuck open and there were people sitting around on the chairs beside a freshly lit fire.

'Don't look at them,' Dad said.

I kept my head down. I was used to doing that. But I couldn't resist a quick glimpse. I wanted to know why he was so determined to ignore the caravan and the people that lived in it.

I flicked my eyes to one side and saw a boy with bright green eyes. He stared right at me, unmoving. It was like he could see something else, something that I wasn't aware of.

I had managed to escape boys looking at me all day. I had played the part of a regular holidaymaker really well—perfectly, in fact. Nobody had bothered me at all.

But the boy by the caravan was too idle, just like the boys at home. He could see everything. I knew it. It would only be a matter of time before the cruel names started again.

'Keep away from them, Star,' Dad said. 'I mean it. They're wanderers.'

'I'd heard talk about them a few days ago,' said Shuna. 'I'd hoped it wasn't true. Such a shame—I wanted you to be able to relax here.'

I had never heard people called wanderers before. I took it to mean: people who wandered from place to place without a real home. Lost people. That made me feel a bit sad.

Everybody deserved a place to call home.

I looked back over my shoulder.

The boy with green eyes was still staring. Looking right at me. Silver rings flashed on his fingers as he pushed his dark fringe back. The look on his face hadn't faltered.

I snapped my head away quickly. I could feel my cheeks burning.

I would definitely stay away from him.

Shuna made pan haggerty for dinner. My favourite. It had been years since I had eaten that. I wolfed it down as we sat around the table in the garden, listening to the residual buzz of a long summer's day. The evening noise, as thick as fire smoke, added density to what had all day been fresh and light.

Soon, the stars returned to remind me where I was—to remind me that the world was more than the estate and the boys at school.

'There are those who can read the night sky,' said Shuna. 'The fae folk say our destiny is already written in the stars.' She stood up from her chair and began to clear the table, a smile spreading across her face.

'Shuna's told me she has a car,' Dad said, quickly changing the subject. 'There's a lot more to see than the beach.

I don't know about fae folk—she's a total fantasist, my sister—but there are a few other places to go. We'll be here for the whole summer—if you want to be.'

I nodded.

'Good,' he said.

Beadnell was a world away from the estate. I felt like I was in the place I was meant to be all along—out in the wild, under the stars, with the smell of the sea in the air.

Maybe I really would fit in here. Maybe I was only days away from making new friends. I allowed myself to think so—to believe in that for a moment. I felt my cheeks rise upwards as a smile pushed around the parts of my face that hadn't been pushed around for ages.

'Now, there's a happy face,' said Shuna.

A sudden noise jumped over the garden wall; it was the sound of laughter, carried on the wind. I looked beyond the colourful stones, turned grey by the night, and saw the little caravan illuminated orange by the fire on the ground outside of it. Shadows grew across it, moving and laughing, as smoke spread across the stars like clouds.

I felt funny. Uneasy. I tried my best to ignore them. I tried to listen intently to Shuna's stories. I tried to enjoy the mint-choc-chip Viennetta she brought out for afters. I tried to ignore the dodgy feeling in my stomach that told me things weren't going to go the way I had hoped—that told me I should be worried.

But I couldn't. Obviously. My perfect holiday was tainted. Flawed. Halted before it had even begun by a caravan, and a flash of green eyes, and a boy who had already seen too much.

Four.

I felt like I couldn't relax until he was gone; until I knew he wouldn't be able to see me; until they all went off to wherever wanderers went. Until I knew they would ruin someone else's summer and leave mine alone.

But, seventy-two hours in, the caravan, filthy and covered in scratches, was still digging its wheels into the grass, sinking deeper into the ground. Like a weed, growing roots that held it firmly in place.

Every morning so far, I had looked out of my window, hoping to see just a field—a wide, green, caravan-less field.

Every morning so far, I had been disappointed.

They weren't going anywhere.

I stood up from my bed, yawning so deeply my arms and legs shook. I walked over to the mirror.

A few freckles had awoken on my face, along the bridge of my nose and across my cheeks. Soft, white hairs had appeared around my forehead and down the side of my ear too. I ran my finger along them; my skin felt really smooth.

The sun was starting to change me. I wondered if anybody else would notice the difference. I wondered if being freckly made me look more approachable; I wondered if silky white hairs made me look more like them.

I definitely looked different. That had to mean something. But after seventy-two hours of being in Beadnell, I still hadn't made friends, and I really should have. Boys here weren't like the ones at home; they were soft around the edges, with messy hairdos instead of shaved heads. They weren't a world away from the boys on the estate—boys were boys, after all—but they definitely looked more relaxed. Making friends with them should have been easier.

I wondered if they stayed away because of Dad.

He had been behaving strangely since we arrived. I couldn't help but notice that, for some reason, he kept a really close eye on me here, much closer than he did at home. Even when I was in my bedroom I could feel him near; hear the floorboards creaking in the hallway and see shadows stopping outside of my door.

I had a feeling the caravan on the field had something to

do with it, which made his behaviour even stranger; he didn't have to worry about me staying away from them—they already terrified me.

I opened my bedroom door. 'Good morning, Star,' said Shuna, passing me in a flurry of colour and smells and jangling things. She slipped on a pair of brown boots and stepped into the porch. She held her crinkly purse in her hand. 'I was just about to go to Mr Wilkinson's.'

Every morning so far, she had walked into the village to collect the newspapers from Mr Wilkinson's shop. According to her, it was the hub of the village. 'But since you're awake, perhaps you'd like to go instead?'

Her dark eyes sparkled, waiting for a response from me. I didn't know what to do. She reached into her purse and pulled out a fiver. 'It's just along the alleyway, on the right-hand side,' she said, stepping out of the brown boots. 'He knows my order.'

She handed me the money and jangled past me, humming some tune.

I moved towards the front door and pulled it open, allowing a breeze to rush through the house. It moved dream-catchers and bells and blew away old cobwebs.

I wasn't sure if I was ready to step out on my own. Shuna was sometimes gone for twenty minutes at a time. That meant the shop got busy—it was probably rammed at this time in the morning. I wasn't sure if I was ready to be seen yet, or what I would do if it all went wrong and the boys here were just like the boys at home.

Then I remembered the freckles and the little white hairs. I remembered the smoothness of my skin. I could still feel it on the tips of my fingers, buzzing like wings.

And, more importantly, I remembered what I wanted. I was here to make friends, not hide in my bedroom—that would get me nowhere.

I had to do it. I had been here for seventy-two hours already and made no progress at all. I wanted friends. I wanted laughter. Those things wouldn't just land on my lap. *More's the pity*, I thought. I would have to go out and find them on my own—up the alleyway and into the village.

Today Mr Wilkinson's, tomorrow the world, I told myself as I walked past the giraffe statue and through the front gate.

'So, you're the boy from down south?' said Mr Wilkinson in a chalky voice. 'Shuna's told me all about you.'

His shop was a mess, filled with dust and old smells. He ran probably the smallest post office, café, newsagent and bakery in the world, and he was the only staff member. He was definitely too old for the job, with a severely crooked back, probably from years of standing behind a counter. And osteoporosis.

I felt confused the second I stepped into it. Fruit and veg crowded together in wicker baskets underneath a postcard stand; tins of cat food stood in stacks of three on top of old boxes of sage and onion stuffing mix, and cleaning products nestled amongst the bread rolls and croissants. No wonder Shuna took so long. It probably took her twenty minutes to find what she was looking for.

'Here for the summer?' he continued. 'I don't blame you wanting to get away—I spent some time in the city when I was young, working on the quayside. Nasty place. It chewed me up and spat me out after a couple of years. I suppose it's different when you're from there.'

I resisted the urge to tell him that it wasn't.

'I had something to tell you,' he continued. 'Now, where is it?' He tapped the side of his head with his index finger. I stood in silence, the only noise coming from a clock that ticked a full minute before he spoke again. 'Ah. There's been a mix-up this morning,' he said, finally. 'I haven't got Shuna's usual newspaper—she always orders a national, you see. It'll be here tomorrow. I'm giving her the *Northumberland Gazette*.' He licked his thumb and took a newspaper from a pile on the counter, passing it to me with shaking hands. 'And I've got her usual crusty rolls, as it's Thursday. I've thrown in a few extra—I know she has company.'

I took the plastic bag, filled with enough bread to feed the village, and placed it, along with the folded newspaper, under my arm.

The bell above the door rang.

A group of laughing voices, sharp voices, entered the shop, and the atmosphere changed. Their noise sliced through the dust, smashing the quiet into pieces. My body stiffened, causing me to squish the bread rolls under my arm.

Mr Wilkinson's shop suddenly felt like a dangerous place to be. The mess and confusion went away, sucked out through the door, and a shadow fell over the mismatched groceries until they went too. I could have been anywhere—an alleyway at midnight, or round the back of the bins on the estate.

I turned around slowly.

There were three of them, pressed together, moving together, like they were the same thing; a pack of wolves. Except they weren't grey or brown. They weren't how I expected them to be. They were colourful. Strange. Belly tops, string vests and platform shoes moved towards me, along with brightly coloured hair and dreadlocks and glitter. There was no way they were from Beadnell. You couldn't get clothes like that in Mr Wilkinson's shop—unless they were hidden somewhere amongst the cucumbers.

'Alright, Wilkinson,' said one of them, a girl. She had watery, yellow eyes and curly hair, shaved on the sides. She wore a vest to show off her muscly, tattooed arms. She looked more like a boy—like one of the boys on the estate. But she was definitely a girl; her voice was light and unbroken, and, possibly a bigger giveaway, she was wearing a bra.

Someone clung to her side. They had long, dreadlocked hair in rainbow colours and a black hoop hanging from the middle of their nose. They were really thin, with big brown eyes, and their cheeks were covered in glitter. High-heeled boots ran up their thighs, fastened up the side with a piece of silver ribbon. I think they may have been a boy because they had stubble on their face, but I had never seen a boy like that before.

I couldn't understand any of them; couldn't work them out. There was a wildness about them—a carelessness that easily made them dangerous. But then, they didn't look dangerous—not really—just different.

They moved together, like they were connected by something that other people couldn't see. Bound by some secret thing. They kept their heads close together, chins down, as if they were whispering to each other, though their mouths weren't moving.

'We've just come for bread and milk,' said the third. *A girl*, I thought, although I really wasn't sure. She was older than the others, and glamorous in her way, with short dyed-red hair and big sunglasses that covered most of her face. Her voice was gruff and burnt around the edges, and her tiny, broken teeth were a little bit grey. 'Oh, and fags. Sorry, Star, did you want to get past?' She stepped to one side to let me by.

But I couldn't move.

The sound of my name, coming through her thin lips and moving around her mouth, turned me to stone. I became as rigid as the stand holding the postcards, or the post box outside.

The three of them stared at me; three sets of eyes seeing me, three people who knew me when I knew nothing about them.

'Lambert and Butler, wasn't it?' said Mr Wilkinson.

I looked to the floor and quickly moved past, my ears filled with her burnt voice; filled with my own name, gradually getting louder.

I stopped outside and looked through the window. I never did that. But I had to. I wanted to look again. I wanted to remember them. They were strange people; exciting people—each of them a mixture of boy bits and girl bits, except they weren't girly or boyish, they were just *them*.

There was no way of telling what they were going to do next. They were sort of capable of anything. Untameable. And they knew my name. *Mine*. I didn't know what to do. The inside of my head was filled with mud. And my thoughts waded through it; sank into it, unable to stick around and tell me what was going on.

The girl with red hair turned. She slid her sunglasses down her nose and I saw a flash of fire in her eyes. She looked at me, right at me. Her face began to move in strange ways. Her lips thinned across her grey teeth, and her eyebrows shot up her forehead. She recognised me. I could see my face in her eyes. I could see that she knew things; things I didn't want anyone to know.

I didn't know what to do next. So I ran, as quickly as I could, past the shop window and along the alley until I reached the cottage. I had made a mistake in looking back. Made a mistake in leaving the house at all.

Hadn't I?

When I got back, Dad and Shuna were in the kitchen.

'I don't want you filling his head with all that,' I heard Dad say.

'He's young,' Shuna said. 'There's no harm in it.'

'He's not like other kids. I don't want him getting any funny ideas.'

'Like what?'

'You know—all that fairy crap.'

'Don't be too hard on him,' said Shuna. 'He's lost his—'

'Here's the bread,' I said, walking into the kitchen and holding the rolls out for Shuna to take.

'Morning, Star,' said Dad, in a suddenly higher voice.

'The old dear has given us extra,' said Shuna, holding the bag of rolls in one hand and placing the other on her chest. 'He's so kind. I don't know what this village would do without him.'

I could think of many things the village could do without him, and at a much faster pace. But that didn't matter. I didn't care about how nice or kind or slow Mr Wilkinson was. It wasn't him that had made my trip to the shop unusual. It was *them*—the colourful people, the ones who knew my name.

They were still with me, though the details of their faces—the shapes of their eyebrows, or the spaces between their noses and mouths—had already faded in my head. *That was weird.* I was really good at remembering faces, really good at seeing people's defining parts and logging them for future reference. But I couldn't remember them at all. It was as if I didn't have the tools to remember them, didn't have the capacity to place them anywhere amongst the faces I already knew. As if they couldn't exist to me.

Something spluttered in the pit of my stomach, like an old car exhaust. The strange people in the shop excited me in ways I had never been excited. An ordinary stranger knowing my name was one thing, but *them* knowing my name meant something else.

I walked into the garden.

'Another beach day today, I think,' said Shuna from the kitchen. 'It's going to be a scorcher.'

I took a seat at the table, my head full of twisted thoughts all tangled around each other; tied in knots like a fishing net. I didn't know where to start in smoothing them out.

I liked the beach. I really liked it, actually. But I couldn't think about that now. Something had happened. Something that changed things; that separated me from the summer I'd thought I was going to have.

I could feel it sort of slipping away from me—the smiles, the friendships, the gang of boys with messy hair. They all became light, drawn in faint pencil, blowing away on the breeze. They didn't belong to me anymore; I couldn't have grabbed them back even if I'd wanted to.

I had the people in the shop to thank for that. The

nameless, faceless people.

Knowing that people like that lived in Beadnell—or existed at all—changed things. I didn't know why.

'I thought you'd lost interest already,' said Dad, taking a seat opposite me.

I poured myself a glass of orange juice and began to slowly drink.

I didn't want him to know about them. They were nothing like him; they were colourful and interesting and wild. Things he knew nothing about. Things he hated. If he found out, if he discovered they had seen me and they knew my name, he would never let me out of his sight. And that would be the end of summer.

If I wanted any kind of freedom at all, I would have to make sure I didn't bump into them again—I got the feeling they wouldn't be as easy to escape a second time.

Five.

The beach was busier than I had seen it. The sand was no longer visible, no longer yellow; instead it was covered in every imaginable colour of beach towel and windbreak, like a patchwork quilt had been thrown over it for preservation. The sea was a wild and noisy soup of rubber rings and surfboards. Everything had reached its peak—the heat of the sun, the overpowering smell of coconut-scented sun cream, and the number of people running from towel to towel.

It appeared summer was in full swing, which meant it was time to join in.

We were lucky to find a spot at all, although it was next to the harbour. It was not the best part of the beach—we were right by a set of rocks that stank of stale seaweed. I wasn't happy to be stuck in the shadows while the rest of the world laughed and played music and splashed each other in the sunshine. That wasn't how this was meant to go.

I kicked a pile of dried seaweed out of the way and laid my towel on the sand. It was much colder in the dark. The breeze caused goose bumps to rise on my arms and legs as it carried the sound of laughing voices to me. A shiver crawled up my spine. I didn't know if I would ever get used to that sound. It reminded me of too many bad things.

It came from the end of the pier, where a group of boys—the most I had seen yet—gathered together. I recognised one or two of them from days before. They looked happy, with freckly noses and sparkly teeth, their hair bending in the wind like the golden grass on the dunes.

Boys here were definitely different from the ones on the estate, which gave me a small amount of confidence. They threw their arms around each other when they laughed and hugged each new friend that joined them. I didn't know boys could be so gentle—and to each other. I wondered if their hugs extended to everyone. I wondered if they extended to me.

I sat in the shadows, watching them jump off the harbour wall—one by one landing into the water, one by one climbing up afterwards and being welcomed into the group again by hugs and congratulations and pats on the back. I wished I knew how to get from here to there. They were the perfect image of what my summer should look like, and they were so close. I could almost feel what it was like to be their friend.

'Busy today, isn't it?' said Dad as a group of kids ran past him, sending sand up into the air. 'Suddenly the back garden isn't looking so bad.'

The thought of spending the day in the garden when everybody else was here was enough to propel me forward from my towel. It was as if someone had booted me up the backside. Life was happening here, right here on this beach, and I wanted to be part of it. I had to find a reason to stay. And fast.

Suddenly I was standing, and right by the harbour wall—right by them. It was like I was floating in this weird transitional space, somewhere between the future and the past; between Dad and my new friends, knowing exactly where I wanted to go, and exactly where I didn't, but being in neither place. I had made a shift; I could feel it on my insides. The journey towards them wasn't that long. They weren't unreachable any more; they were right there.

All I had to do was walk. Put one foot in front of the other. Just get there. The rest would follow.

'Where are you going?' asked Dad. I didn't answer, just carried on, my eye on the prize. I was doing it. I was actually doing it.

It was a lot windier up on the harbour wall. I hadn't expected that. The sea on the other side was wild, diving into jagged black rocks and spraying high into the air, fizzing in all directions like an exploding bottle of coke. I hadn't expected that either.

I looked over the edge. It was really far down—double my height.

I wasn't that good at swimming. I had stopped going to the city pool with school as soon as I was allowed to drop out because I hated being seen in my swimming shorts and hated changing with the other boys.

Actually, I was glad I had, because Naseera told me that soon after, at the start of year eight, our class started doing silly tasks instead of learning to swim. Things like retrieving rubber blocks from the bottom of the pool in their pyjamas. Ridiculous. So, as it turned out, I wouldn't have worn my swimming shorts if I had stayed on anyway. I would have ruined a pair of pyjamas, though, so all in all, I was glad I hadn't gone back.

I was starting to think I should have now, though; starting to think that ruining an old pair of pyjamas would have been worth the bother.

All my time spent watching at my bedroom window had given me a slight advantage in that I knew exactly how boys worked. There was only one way to get in with them, and that was to appeal to their ego—their pride—the part that made them tense their arms and lift their chests and laugh really loudly so everyone could hear, especially when they were grouped together.

If I wanted to make friends, I had to join the race; prove I was a worthy competitor; do exactly what the others did. It was either that or look back on a summer spent in the back garden, with Dad.

And I didn't want that.

I placed one foot in front of the other, moving towards them, approaching with caution. None of them turned around. That was good. My heart began to punch me in the ribs. Every new beat jolted my shoulders forward, knocking the breath out of me.

Come on, Star. Get a hold of yourself, I whispered. I only had one chance to make a first impression—to be one of the boys. Any whiff of difference and I was out.

I decided to leave my t-shirt on. The other boys were built like boys were supposed to be—perfectly square in places and lean in others. I wasn't like that. I had rounded shoulders and hips. They wouldn't accept me if they saw that. I had to appear as much like them as possible.

I tied my hair at the nape of my neck and tucked it under

my shirt so it looked short. That was important. Boys didn't have long hair.

Then, I took as deep a breath as I could, and I ran like I was running for my life.

My feet thudded against the harbour wall, shaking the bones in my legs, jolting my knees. The wind grabbed my hair and set it free from its prison under my t-shirt. I felt it spring upwards and flap at the back of my neck. It was too late to stop it; too late to do anything except run and jump and fly.

And fall.

Seeing the water—the hugeness of it—threw me off. I sort of half chickened out and half really went for it, resulting in a kind of flailing belly flop thing. I think. I smacked into the sea on my side. My skin stung as seawater flushed into my nose and ears, burning them with salt.

I disappeared into a cloud of bubbles. All of the sounds and smells of summer vanished in an instant. I was in pain from the fall but somehow at the same time in a painless state; held in cold, salty space.

I tried to move my arms and legs, but they weren't mine anymore. They started to flounce of their own accord like jelly by my side. I kicked but nothing happened. That was weird. It happened again. My body began to spasm. I was sort of swimming, definitely moving, but at the same time, not. If anything, I was going in the wrong direction, sinking deeper rather than moving upwards. I could feel the water getting colder around my feet.

My chest felt really light, and for the first time in as long as I could remember, I felt calm. Like I wasn't me. Like someone else had taken over and all I had to do was let them. That felt nice. There was no such thing as heavy here; it couldn't exist. The water cancelled it out. I just floated, in silence; down, down, down, held in a moment, where all the things that made life hard couldn't get to me.

Baby, said Mam's voice. She was laughing—my favourite sound in the world. *Hello, baby*, she said. I could see her—really see her this time—swimming right next to me.

I reached out to touch her, to grab her arm, to feel the smoothness of her skin.

Suddenly, a hand came through the cloud of bubbles, gripping my hair and nipping my skin, before finally holding the back of my t-shirt and pulling me upwards.

The brightness of sunlight stung my eyes awake as I burst into a world of noise, coughing up a rush of salty water. It burned hot and sharp as it left my body. Somewhere above, I could hear them, killing themselves with laughter, their voices turned from kind to cruel, echoing through the limekilns and around the harbour.

The hand pulled me around the harbour wall until my heels collided with the seabed.

I scrambled up to my feet, my body shaking all over without me telling it to. I wiped my eyes with my fingers and took as deep a breath as I could.

'You can't swim,' said a voice. A boy. 'Why the hell would you do that if you can't swim?' The boy with green eyes stood in the shallows, fully clothed and dripping wet. 'I've never seen anything so stupid in my life,' he said. 'Jumping off a pier when you can't swim.'

I could swim. Just not well enough, apparently.

'You could've drowned,' he continued. He was angry. 'And that lot wouldn't have saved you—they were laughing.'

I continued to cough. I couldn't take a deep enough breath. The salt had nearly squeezed my throat closed. I felt light-headed, like I might pass out or throw up. Stars danced around the corners of my eyes, running in circles, flashing like lights.

I needed this boy to go away, to leave me alone, but he continued to stare at me. Waiting for a response. He would never get one. The reality of what had happened began to gnaw at my stomach, just under my heart. Scratching away at my insides like a parasite that fed off my shame—getting fatter by the second. I had made a complete fool of myself in front of every boy in Beadnell. I had screwed up big time. He should have left me to drown.

'You're an idiot,' he said, before running past me and diving back into the sea.

I watched him swim around the wall and disappear from sight, probably to join in the laughter with the others.

I slumped down in the shallows, my head lolloping up and down as my breaths steadied. I was an idiot—as well as a fairy, and a freak, and all the other horrible names that were bound to follow this. I had played it completely wrong. I had gambled with my only chance of friendship and lost everything.

I slapped my hand off my forehead and squeezed it. Pain began to peck at my temples, like it always did when I was embarrassed or hopeless or sad. That literally could not have gone any worse. Even if I had drowned, I would have been oblivious to the laughter, to the teasing and to all the other horrible things that I could still hear coming from the end of the harbour wall.

I was going to be known as the idiot who jumped off the pier but couldn't swim. The half-gadge who almost drowned—who couldn't even get swimming right. There was no chance they would accept me now.

What a Shiloh Pitt.

I never wanted to go to the beach ever again. The thought of even one person recognising me, or laughing at me, was enough to send me off on a one-boy mission into the depths of my head.

I closed the windows and drew the curtains, shutting out all light so I could fester in the darkness. I wanted it. I was sick and tired of pretending I didn't. Sick and tired of trying to make friends, trying to be happy, trying to be anything other than what I really was—damaged and brittle and dark. There was no point in pretending otherwise.

I had spent a lifetime watching. Trying my hardest to observe every detail and learn how to be more like everyone else. I had studied their mannerisms and clothes and hairstyles. I had listened to their conversations. But still, even after all of that, even after a lifetime of trying as hard as I could, I was still me.

I felt horrible, like an army of ants were crawling over my skin. I couldn't settle. I felt so desperate. I wanted to hold on to something, to hold someone, to hold her. I needed her now. This had gone on for far too long.

I tried to imagine her. I tried to hear her voice, see her eyes. Smell her hair.

But it didn't work like that. That's what she had said. She came whenever she needed to. Not when I needed her to.

And I was still angry. And it was still happening. And this was still my life.

I felt the dark cloud; her dark cloud, moving up my back and creeping over my head until it hung just above my eyebrows, just enough to box me in.

I wondered how dark the cloud had to be before it took over and I lost control, like her. I wondered if she thought of me at all, if she loved me at all. I found it hard to see how she could.

The noise in my head grew louder. I began to panic. My legs shook, my fingers curled inwards, stiffened in fists. *Louder.* But I couldn't stop. I was losing control. *Louder.* I was so scared. My ears burned so hot that I wrapped my arms around my head. *Louder.* Pain tore through the left-hand side of my chest, through to my back.

Next thing I knew, I was on the carpet. It scratched my cheek as I lay on my side, cold and still.

One minute passed.

One hour passed.

One night passed: one starless, hopeless, motherless night.

Baby, she said. I knew she would come. She was the only one who cared about me. The only one who knew what I needed. *Go outside, baby*, she said. Her eyes were bigger than usual, but still as alive as I remembered them. Her hair moved around her face, as if it wasn't made from thousands of tiny strands, but one thing: space, the stuff in between the stars.

The universe grew from her pretty head. Stars danced in her eyes. Worlds began by her words. She was the architect of everything that I was. *Enjoy the sun*, she said again. *It's summertime.*

I wanted to. Even after everything, I still wanted to. That amazed me. My hopes wouldn't leave me.

'Stay,' I said. It would be easier with her.

She began to move and change, fading into the shadows of my bedroom, into the creases in the curtains, into the gap between the wardrobe and the wall.

'Stay,' I said again.

'Sorry?' said Shuna. Her deep, booming voice vibrated in my chest and shocked me awake.

She stood in the doorway, her smiling face tilted to one side.

The grey clouds of my dreams still clung to the edges of my bedroom, softening the corners as if my bed, the chair beside it, and my crumpled-up clothes hanging over it weren't really there.

But Shuna definitely was. Her bright eyes fixed on me, waiting for something.

I focused on her from my position on the floor, until my head cleared. Until I could be sure of where I was. It took some time.

'I won't let you do it,' she said after a minute, 'not here. Summers are to be spent outdoors—in the sunshine. You'll thank me for this one day.'

She disappeared behind the door but left it wide open.

Her words hung in the room, made of thin smoke, as if they had grown from the end of one of her incense sticks. Though they didn't smell as sweet.

I sat up and caught my reflection in the mirror. I was no longer sun-tanned and freckly. I looked gaunt and grey and creased. I had finally turned into Dad. I sat for a minute, gathering my thoughts, as if they were dirty laundry on the floor.

I knew she was right. I knew summers were supposed to be spent outdoors. *Go outside*. That's what Mam said.

But I didn't know how to do it on my own. I seemed to make mistakes at every turn; ruin things that I was trying to make better. *How could a person manage to get everything so spectacularly wrong?* It was like every good intention I had turned to dust in my hands. Ashes. I could almost taste them on my tongue, making it hard to swallow; hard to breathe.

Every time I ventured out, I was reminded of what I was. I didn't know how to change that. I needed help. I needed someone to guide me through. A voice in the shadows, that came and went as easily as the breeze, wasn't enough. I needed someone real, someone I could cling to and rely upon; someone who could pull me out of the dark—heave me upwards—before I sank too far into it to be rescued.

I walked into the kitchen. Shuna's face was concerned. Her tiny, sparkling eyes turned down at the edges. 'I still haven't been for the bread this morning,' she said. 'I know you like to do that.' I didn't like to. Not anymore. 'I always feel better getting out of the house. Just being out there can lift my spirits when I don't know how to myself.' She winked at me, holding out a fiver. 'Give it a go.'

I took the note and shuffled into the hallway and out of the front door.

Then I was on the road. Outside felt no different to inside. It didn't matter where I was. A hole had opened up somewhere inside of me and I had fallen through. That's where I was. That's where I would stay—right at the bottom. Indoors, outdoors, it made no difference at all.

Then I was in the alleyway, my feet scraping across the

flattened mud and gravel. I could hear raised voices at the end, but I didn't stop; didn't think to quietly pace backwards and run in the opposite direction, as if I hadn't been there at all. As if I didn't exist at all. I couldn't be bothered to pretend. My instincts had dulled to a whisper. Raised voices didn't scare me anymore.

'Puff,' someone said. A boy.

'Look at the state of him,' said another one. 'When was the last time you had a proper wash, pikey?'

'His lot don't wash, man.'

Two boys, huge, with red faces, had someone up against the side of the shop window. They leant in close, spitting with every nasty word that hissed through their gritted teeth.

I watched. Not brave enough to stop them, but not scared enough to run. Changed, but not changed enough. All I could do was stand and wait until they saw me.

'Here's another one,' said one of them, noticing me. 'Another pikey, mate—is it a lad or a lass, though?'

His words didn't even poke me in the shoulder. Didn't touch me at all. I was so bored of hearing the same thing all the time. So bored of the same angry faces. There was nothing particular about this breed—they were the boys on the backfield in bigger tracksuits. That was all. *Couldn't they think of something original to say?* I felt like I lived in a world of clones and that I was from another planet entirely—one where the difference between boys and girls wasn't half as wide and mattered even less than that.

Someone brushed past me and knocked me forward. Knocked me closer to them, close enough to smell the salty sweat on their clothes. 'Alright,' she said. It was the girl with dyed-red hair. 'Party is over. Sling your hook before you have to deal with me.'

'And what are you?' said one of them.

'I'm your worst nightmare, lads—a woman with a mind of her own.'

She took a drag of her cigarette and blew thick smoke into their faces. She walked towards them, her head tilted back, jugular exposed. She was formidable. Fearless.

'We're not finished with you lot,' said one of them. He looked right at me. 'Look at this fairy.'

'Aye, very nice,' said the girl, 'now be a good little troglodyte and run along. There's a good lad.'

One of them spat on the ground. 'Gypsy scum,' they said, before walking away.

The girl turned to me and smiled. 'Are you okay, Star?'

The sound of my own name, spoken in that voice, cracked the fog in my head; snapped me out of whatever trance I was in. I had totally forgotten about her—forgotten that she knew my name.

'Ignore them if you can,' she continued. 'People like that don't like folk like us—never have, never will. It's just one of those things. Nothing worth worrying about, babes.'

Folk like us. She was including me in that. I think. *Folk like us*. But I was nothing like her. I wished I was. She was strong and bright and quick. *Folk like us.* No one had ever tried to include me. I had never been picked.

But she didn't seem to know that. Or if she did, she didn't care about it.

She walked towards me and placed her hand on my arm. She smelt warm, like smoke mixed with almond oil. It clung to her coarse hair and clothes. 'I'm glad I've bumped into you,' she said. 'I wondered if you could do something for me.'

I didn't move. Just stared. I felt like I had left my body and I was watching myself from above, as if I were standing on the harbour wall looking down at the water, as if I hadn't jumped yet. As if the last twenty-four hours hadn't happened.

'Will you come to the beach tonight?' she asked. 'I heard you went for a swim with Benji yesterday. Come and talk to him—it'll do you good. You don't have to be on your own all of the time, Star.'

There it was again: my name. It sounded so unusual spoken by her—interesting instead of weird, like she said it the way it was supposed to be said. Like she understood. Like she knew exactly who I was. I wondered if she could tell me; if she could help me out of the mess I was in. I had a feeling she could. Something told me that's what she did.

I couldn't do what she asked, though. I couldn't talk to the boy. He was just like all the rest of them; another laughing face to add to the crowd. He had called me an idiot. Why would I want to talk to him? I hated him.

The girl walked over to the window. The boy with long dreadlocks lay on the ground. He was smiling, which seemed really strange considering what had just happened. She stroked his face with her long fingers—finished with blood red nails—and he pressed his cheek against her hand, like a dog or a cat does when its owner strokes it.

They really were so different to anyone else I had met—they had their own way of reacting to things, like they felt things differently and weren't afraid to show it. There was no way they came from Beadnell. They were far too exotic, far too strange and interesting. Beadnell was many things, but, I had come to realise, strange and interesting it was not.

I knew they were from somewhere else, but it hadn't occurred to me just how far away that place could be. And if they knew him, if they knew the boy from the caravan, then it made sense that they were from the caravan too.

They weren't just people—they were *wanderers*.

This changed things. There was no way I was going to the beach with a bunch of wanderers. They were bad people—dangerous—they could have done anything to me. Plus Dad would be furious if he ever found out.

I had to get away from them.

'Think about it,' said the girl with red hair. 'I just saved your backside there. You owe me a favour.' She smiled with her grey, pointed teeth. 'We'll be at the harbour end.'

She put her arm around the boy with the dreadlocks and kissed him on the cheek. Then they walked off down the alley and disappeared, leaving me to stare at my blank reflection in the window of Mr Wilkinson's shop.

Six.

I didn't go. I still hadn't recovered from the episode on the end of the pier. *Watergate*, I liked to call it. I definitely wasn't strong enough to mess things up again.

So I kept a low profile; surrendered my summer to Dad—to boredom and quiet, and all the things he enjoyed. Time was spent in the local pub, watching the sports channels. Or inside the grey walls of the back garden, watching his frowning face occasionally watching me with—more often than not—sad eyes.

I became tired; a shadow of the person I really wanted to be, floating from one place I didn't really want to go to another, like a cloud. A ghost. Controlled by something else. Controlled by him.

My only excitement came in the evenings, when the

wanderers lit their fire on the beach. I would watch the smoke from my bedroom window, rising over the dunes, the smell of burnt leaves floating to me, filling my head with voices and colours as the flames spat out orange stars that danced away on a black wind.

Knowing who they were made them realer to me—made them more than a broken caravan, or a scary group of people. In a strange way, I felt connected to them. I would hear my name, rolling across the field, spoken in a voice that made sense of it. Made sense of me; untangled me and pointed me in the right direction.

I couldn't forget the way the girl with dyed-red hair made me feel. She gave me a sense of belonging. She spoke to different parts of my body; I heard her in my stomach and in my bones as well as in my ears. *Folk like us.* That's what she said, like I was one and the same. Like I was a wanderer too.

As the days passed by in a constant stream of *Match of the Day* and chips with curry sauce, and the nights in a whirlwind of heavy smoke and stars, I started to think I had made the wrong decision and surrendered my summer to the wrong team.

I slowly became obsessed by the voices that came to me in the night. I began to feel like they were calling me to them—pulling some invisible chord, as fine as cobwebs, attached to my insides; maybe calling back the favour I owed, as if it were more than just an act of kindness. As if the girl with red hair had left something with me that carried a price.

Day-by-day, hour-by-hour, it became heavier. I felt like I was wearing a straitjacket made of heavy wool; unable to move properly, unable to think. I wanted to take it off. I wanted to be released from whatever debt I owed.

I sort of knew the only way to repay it would be to do what she asked: to go to the beach at night and talk to the boy with green eyes. But doing that seemed impossible.

There was something else, too—I couldn't remember their faces. They were more feeling to me than memory. Every flutter of the wings in my belly, every rush of blood to the moving parts of me, I could recall straight away. I remembered the way they moved; the way their chins stayed low and close to each other; the way it felt like they were whispering to each other even when their mouths were still. But their faces were lost somewhere in my mind.

It was so strange, like I wasn't allowed to remember the details. All I could see was green eyes, reflecting the copper sunset like a new penny; or shiny hair falling over tanned skin; or red hair and smoke-stained teeth.

They weren't things that made up a face. They weren't individual to them; they were additional things, things that came later. Anyone could smoke, or dye their hair red, and loads of people had green eyes. It was noses and mouths and the spaces in between them that made people who they were; it was eyelashes and shadows and lines that made up a face.

I couldn't remember any of that, no matter how much time I spent trying.

'You're quiet tonight,' said Dad one evening over dinner.

I had been thinking about them. Again. I forced a smile across my face, like I always did. I didn't think I was any quieter than usual. I never really spoke to him about my secrets, and I absolutely knew I couldn't tell him about this one. He had made his feelings about the people who lived in the caravan very clear.

'Your eyes look dark,' he said. 'What about the beach tomorrow—for a change?'

It wouldn't be a change. There was no change. Time spent with him was the same wherever we were—at home or in Beadnell. He somehow managed to make the sun less bright and the stars less twinkly. I felt tired around him. Adding this to the weight of the favour I owed the girl with red hair, I felt like I could barely move.

I wanted to be free of him. Free of everything. Just like them.

I allowed myself to wonder what would happen if I just

did it: if I just threw caution to the wind and followed the black smoke to the beach.

A scenario unravelled in my head like a ball of wool, and I watched it unfold, surprised at what I saw; a night spent under the stars, surrounded by like-minded people and stories. Surrounded by friends.

The hummingbirds returned to my belly, filling it up with movement and energy, and, just like that, I knew what I had to do.

'I'm going to bed,' I said, standing up from the table without really thinking about it. 'Yep. Bed.' It was as if my body had made a decision, and my mind needed a second or two to catch up.

'But you haven't finished,' said Dad. 'Sit down and finish your tea.' I didn't look at him. Didn't stop. I had already turned my back; was already walking towards the kitchen. 'Star,' he called after me. 'Star.'

I sat on the side of my bed, my body still as ice but my insides sparking like flames. There really was nothing stopping me from going to the beach.

Strangely, the reasonable voice inside my head wasn't doing what I expected it to; it was barely a whisper—maybe saying something about staying safe or hiding under the covers, but in a totally non-committal kind of a way. It was like even *that*—even the voice of reason inside of me—had grown tired of sports channels and sadness; had grown tired of such a riskless summer. Like it had been rendered null and void.

Without that voice telling me to run the other way, the choice I had to make was clear.

I moved the chair from the end of my bed and pushed it against the door handle. Then I stared out of the window at the setting sun and the field, at the grass and the dunes and the blue forever. This felt different. New. I was falling, but towards a very definite target.

If I had known it would feel so easy, I would have done it much sooner.

I climbed onto the windowsill, gripping it with my hands like a magpie on a telephone wire, still waiting for a thought to form. Still waiting for reason to take hold. Still waiting to be told *no*.

But there was nothing. I was on my own. This choice had to be all mine. I had to lay claim to whatever came next.

Fly or fall.

By the time I got to the beach, the sky was dark. A smudge of broken clouds sat above the dunes, their underbellies scratched and bleeding red as the sun set somewhere over the mountains.

My head felt surprisingly clear. I had forgotten how beautiful the bay was; how the water looked like liquid silver, how it mirrored the sky. I didn't feel as scared as I thought I would. Where I had expected to hear cruel laughter, there was only the sound of shallow waves smoothing across the sand, quietly turning it to glass.

In the distance, people walked along the water's edge. They looked tiny against the stretching bay, like twigs caught up in a picnic blanket.

'Hello,' said someone behind me.

It was the boy with green eyes. He stood in the dunes, a cigarette tucked behind his ear and his curly hair hanging over his face like ribbons.

And then I remembered. I felt stupid that I had ever forgotten. A face like his was unusual. Unique. I should have been able to recall it whenever I wanted to. I should have been able to see the groove in his chin, or his thick eyelashes, or the freckle on the corner of his top lip. 'You came,' he said.

I folded my arms, my mouth sort of twisting into a smile. The last thing I needed was an altercation with him. I wasn't strong enough for his words. Last time we met he had called me an idiot.

'Can't you talk?'

I could feel my cheeks burning. I opened my mouth to speak. Nothing came out. My tongue had swollen to twice its original size. It lay heavy and motionless on the floor of my mouth, like a stone.

'Aren't you going to tell me your name?' he asked.

Don't mess it up.

'Stalin,' I mumbled. I think.

What the hell?

'Stalin?' he repeated, his voice decorated with amusement. 'Should I be worried?' He had come to torture me. I could tell.

'Star,' I said.

'Star. That's better. I don't know if I've ever met a Star. I'm Benji.'

He looked at me. Waiting. He wanted something in return. I had nothing.

'You're so strange,' he said.

Here we go.

He looked me up and down, and all I could do was stand there and let him. I was powerless: a caged bird, voiceless, tormented and trapped. I existed only for his amusement. I wanted to fly away from him. I was weird, and he was so confident and forthcoming—the things a boy was supposed to be. He was earth and roots, solid and present, and I was just air, floating around him, to be used and manipulated.

'Aren't you going to say hello to me?' he asked.

'H …' I began. 'Hello.'

He tilted his head back and laughed, flashing his white teeth. He was so healthy. So functioning; so alive. He carried on talking, but I couldn't hear him. My mind began to wander, following a trail of tiny dark hairs that ran shimmering and smooth down his neck to the bone at the top of his spine.

Boys always had really thick, silky skin—smooth like a peach, but durable.

He reached out a strong hand and grabbed my wrist, wrapping me in warmth, pulling me towards him into the long grass. 'Come with me,' he said.

I didn't know how to stop him—didn't know what to do at all. A boy had never pulled me towards them, only pushed me away, or kicked me to the ground, and I didn't think he was going to do that.

He turned around and I saw he was wearing fairy wings, pink and sparkly, made from net, like the kind you could buy in the Disney store. I didn't think boys could wear things like that, but he wore them proudly just the same. That sort of confused me, softened me—made me more pliable for him. *Why was he wearing fairy wings?*

He led me further into the dunes, carefully guiding me to wherever we were going. He danced between green needles as lightly as a paper bag in the wind, as if the breeze blew under his feet—as if his Disney-wings were real wings. He flitted and swapped, climbed up and jumped down, and I followed in his footsteps, too scared to do anything else.

We reached the highest point, and the long grass parted. Below, there was an opening, surrounded by tall dunes on all sides. A den. In the middle, a shallow fire flickered over a couple of thick logs. Around it sat a group of people holding beer cans and smoking cigarettes and laughing with each other.

It was *them*—the wanderers. My spine became as rigid as the mast of a sailing boat. I was walking right into the dragons' den. *What the hell was I thinking?* I grabbed onto his wrist and tried to pull him off. 'Don't be scared,' he said. He wouldn't let go. He squeezed me tighter. I tried to pull back. I was making a huge mistake. 'They don't bite.'

He led me down to the fire and I followed quietly, hoping they wouldn't notice me arrive.

'Here they are,' said someone.

'Everyone,' Benji began, 'this is Star. Star—meet Jordan, Shea, and of course, you know Kitty.'

'He's young,' said someone else, 'jail bait.'

The group laughed, and my face burned hotter than the fire.

‘Oh, leave him alone,’ said the girl with red hair. ‘He’s just a baby puppy.’ She threw her arms around me and squeezed. ‘I’m glad you came. That shows courage. Come and sit by me.’ Her eyes were really unusual. They twisted and changed colour, like engine oil on a puddle, red one minute and yellow the next, always moving.

‘Do you want a drink?’ asked Benji, opening a can.

I shook my head.

‘A cigarette?’ asked Kitty.

I shook my head again.

‘He’s a good little jail bait,’ said the girl with shaved hair.

I recognised her from the shop. The boy with the long dreadlocks sat next to her, resting his head on her shoulder. He had a bruise along one side of his face. He threw me a smile, but nothing more.

‘Shut up, Shea,’ said Benji, looking at her. Then he leant in closer to me and whispered in my ear. ‘I’m glad you came.’

His words made their way down my back like warm water, and I felt my spine soften. I dared to look at him. Dared to look into his eyes. He smiled. No one had ever smiled at me before. Not like that.

‘How long will you be here, Baby Puppy?’ asked Kitty.

I felt the words rising. If the wanderers didn’t think I was strange to look at, they would definitely laugh when they heard my voice. Everyone did. *For Pete's sake, Star, don't mess it up*, I thought. 'A few more weeks,' I said. My words lingered in the air for a second, just above the fire. Everything seemed to stop. Part of me wished I could have grabbed them back. Part of me wished I could have had another chance to get it right—to sound more normal.

'That's good,' she said. 'And it's just the three of you?'

I nodded.

'Use words,' Benji said. 'Always words.'

'Yes,' I said.

'It's good to have you here,' she said.

She didn't react to my voice as if I was strange or girly or light. None of them did.

Benji offered me his can and I took a sip. The beer warmed my stomach. I had to throw my hand over my mouth to conceal a burp.

Kitty threw a fistful of grass onto the fire. I recognised the smell instantly. It was their smell; burnt herbs and smoke and salt wind. I had come to associate it with excitement, with adventure, with longing for things I wasn't allowed. Now I was there, beside them, I felt those things even more strongly.

The smoke rose slowly, and Kitty looked through it, as if she could see things the rest of us couldn't. She stretched her neck and moved her head from side to side, watching something play out, moving to the rhythm of the flames.

She walked around it, whispering something, drawing a circle in the sand with her foot and dropping a trail of crystals and stones behind her into the groove. The crystals fell like stars, glistening in the firelight; glowing from within as if the flames were trapped inside. The smoother, duller stones had holes in the middle. The fire flashed through them as they fell. I lost myself staring at them, drinking the beer, listening to Kitty chant, and searching the lights within the lights.

Benji seemed to want to be closer to me. I never thought anyone would come near me again. I felt like closeness and touching were things that happened between other people; real people—and I wasn't like other people, so I couldn't have those things. I thought Mam had taken them with her.

It didn't stop me wanting them, though; it didn't stop me wishing for them every time I stared out of my bedroom window at the other families on the estate. Maybe that was just as important.

'So, are you gay?' asked Shea.

'No,' I said automatically. *What the hell—who asks things like that?*

'Shea!' said Benji.

'Stop!' said Kitty.

'What?' said Shea, 'I was only asking.'

‘He’s just got here,’ said Kitty. ‘You barely know him.’

‘Honestly, guys,’ said Shea, ‘it’s really not that bad a question.’

‘Obviously not for you,’ said Benji. ‘But it might be for Star. Just ignore her,’ he said, turning to me. ‘She’s got no filter.’

‘Jealous?’ she said.

‘I don’t need a filter,’ said Benji.

‘Said no one, ever,’ said Jordan.

If my face was burning before, it was probably incinerated by now. The question had come out of nowhere. I felt like the girl with the shaved hair, Shea, had pulled the beach out from under me and I was falling through nothing. It had all just escalated really quickly. And just as quickly, the conversation turned. They were arguing one minute and joking the next. I couldn’t keep up.

‘You’re obviously something,’ said Shea.

‘It’s none of your business,’ said Benji.

‘Can’t he talk for himself?’

‘You’re being rude now.’

‘I’m asking a civilised question.’

‘There’s nothing civilised about you.’

‘Sorry ’bout it,’ she said, flicking her hand.

It happened again. They were arguing, then they were

joking. It was like nothing was worth taking seriously.

Was Shea really asking me? Did I really have to answer? Was there an initiation into this group that involved over-sharing on the first meeting?

I couldn't answer her because, really, I wasn't sure.

I wasn't an idiot. I knew I wasn't like other boys. Like Shea said, I must have been *something*. But no one had ever asked me, no one had ever allowed me to think like that—I had been led to believe that it was scary or weird or wrong.

I didn't know if I fancied other boys. Most of the time they annoyed me; that's if they weren't laughing at me. Did I fancy girls? No, definitely not. That ruled out bisexual—didn't it? I was starting to feel stupid.

I felt like I had to use a part of my brain that, up until that moment, had been off-limits. I didn't know where to start. I didn't know how to navigate my way around all of the muddy grey matter. It was limp and useless, as fragile as a baby. It needed to be strengthened.

'I don't know,' I said.

'Oh, give me a break, Jail Bait,' said Shea. 'Of course you know. Everyone knows.'

'I really don't,' I said. 'I've never met anyone who's gay—'

'You have now,' said Shea.

'You're being crass, Shea,' said Kitty. 'And I, for one, don't want to hear it any more.'

'I'm not,' said Shea.

'Yes, you are,' Kitty said. 'You know we don't play by those rules.'

That seemed to do it. Kitty seemed to hold some sort of authority amongst them. She was older. Thank god I had her on side.

'You're young, Star,' she said, turning to me. 'Be free. Be kind to yourself. The journey to knowing thyself starts with kindness.'

'You don't have to answer,' said Benji, waving his hands. 'Don't think you're going to get the Spanish Inquisition every time you come here. Shea's just a wind-up merchant.'

'Excuse me,' said Shea. 'I resemble that remark.'

'Don't you mean resent?' said Benji.

'I know what I mean.'

She looked right at me, holding me in her cool gaze for more than an awkward moment. I could see, though she may have dismissed her question as a joke, that this was important to her. She didn't let just anyone into the group. She reminded me of a stray cat that wouldn't be stroked—a wild animal that had been spurned too many times. I got this protective feeling from her, like she cared about the people around the fire very much and didn't want anyone to get too close to them. Four was enough for her. They didn't need a fifth. I looked at the bruise on Jordan's face and understood why she felt that way.

People hadn't been kind to them because they were different. I knew exactly how that felt, and if I ever wanted to come back I had to let her know that.

'I don't mean any harm,' I said.

'Of course not,' said Kitty. 'We know that, Star.'

'I …' I began, 'I just want you all to know that.'

That wasn't how it was meant to come out, but my mouth became too dry to speak again.

The conversation hopped and ran to other places as Benji and Kitty tried to move away from Shea's interrogation of the new boy.

But I was left behind. Thinking.

Ultimately, I would have to answer her question, which left me wondering—*what was I?*

It shouldn't have been rocket science. I really should have known myself well enough to answer. But, until tonight, I hadn't met anyone as free as the wanderers. People like them didn't live on the estate, and they certainly didn't go to my school. I had no one to compare myself to. I was just me, Star, the only one. A boy who looked like a girl, who maybe fancied boys but wasn't really sure, and who didn't really know if he was actually a boy because he was so different to the other boys.

It was safe to assume that I was more than a little bit complicated.

But one thing I kind of knew was that, whatever I turned out to be, it was okay to be it with them. There were no judgements. Shea may have been goading me, but at the same time, it weirdly felt like she was encouraging me to uncover who I really was.

Benji's thumb began to massage the back of my neck. 'You're still thinking about it, aren't you?' he said.

'No,' I answered.

'You are,' he said. 'It's fine. Shea can be a pain in the neck when she wants to be. Don't worry about it too much.'

'I'm not,' I said again. I didn't want him to think I was sensitive. I didn't want him to see any of my flaws, actually, which was weird.

I had gone from fearing the very sight of him, to hating him, to now actually liking him. That was even weirder. I never moved that quickly—there was no one else I knew who held a grudge like me. I liked to mull over things, think about every last detail until I was exhausted, and then think some more.

But they didn't have time for that. They liked to get to the point. They didn't waste time on all the stuff in the middle—the thinking and waiting and thinking again. They acted as soon as they felt and then they moved on.

That's what made them so dangerous.

I could see why other people feared them, why Dad told me to stay away. He hated emotions. He hated things he couldn't control, and the people sitting around the fire were completely untameable.

For a split second, I allowed myself to think that maybe I was too, and for the first time in forever, I could hear the murmurs of a forgotten voice coming from somewhere inside of me, like I was remembering the person I was before; the happy, confident, funny kid who didn't have much to carry through life. Who didn't yet know about the darkness of the past few years.

I was suddenly human again. Valuable. Equal. My voice was just as important. I was worthy of the same stuff as everyone else, and no less.

I couldn't ignore how brilliant that felt.

When the flames had died, Kitty collected the stones from the ground. She dropped them, one by one, into a golden bag, inspecting each one before letting it go.

She twisted one around in her hand, holding it between her blood red nails. 'You take this one,' she said. It was a small, smoothed stone with a hole in the middle. It looked like one of the stones from Shuna's cottage, except without the fluorescent paint. Still, I didn't feel comfortable taking anything from her. I knew how it felt to owe her something. 'A holey stone,' she said, 'to remember this night.'

I shook my head.

She held it in the palm of her hand. For a moment I thought I could see the fire through the hole, as if it were burning inside. As if it were trapped in there. 'It's not your choice to make, I'm afraid,' she said. 'This one has chosen you.' She spoke about it like it had a mind of its own. Like it was a living thing. 'Legend says that you can see the fae folk through the hole of a holey stone.'

I searched her face, looking for something that told me she wasn't being serious—a twist of her mouth to conceal a laugh, maybe. I had already learned they followed everything with a joke.

But a joke didn't come. She was as still as the stone in her hand. So I took it from her and placed it in my pocket.

'Keep it with you,' she said.

'Thank you,' I said.

I felt the debt I owed her lift away. We were even. I could

have walked away then and not been troubled by it, or them, again.

But I didn't want to. My mind was already two steps ahead of me—planning how I could see them again.

Benji took my wrist and led me away, through the dunes and over the field. We walked in silence, keeping to the beaten path, past the caravan and slowly towards the shallow grey wall.

'We go to the beach most nights,' he said. 'We don't usually stay anywhere as nice as this, so we're making the most of it—will you meet me tomorrow?'

'Yes,' I said.

'Good—same time tomorrow.'

I pushed the gate open with my foot and walked through the garden. I turned before I reached my bedroom window.

He was already gone.

Seven.

The holey stone lay on my bedroom floor, surrounded by dirty laundry. I watched it through my eyelashes. My tired eyes were not yet awake; my mind not ready to understand how it had got there. All I could do was stare at it and wait for a thought to come, enjoying the smoothness of its curves and the perfect hole in the middle where the fire had been.

My heart began to quicken, slowly guiding me into the morning and away from the night before. My body pulsed—shoulders, stomach and fingertips—and the mattress under me did the same, as if each tiny spring inside was a tiny heart.

I puffed out my chest and sprang forward. I was awake. I was alive. And I suddenly knew exactly why the stone was there—to remind me of it: I had done something brave for the first time in my entire life.

My fists clenched in mid-air. *Yes!* I had answered the call of the wanderers. I had gone to their fire. I had followed the voices that called me on the wind, and it had paid off because I had finally made friends.

My fists clenched again.

Just knowing that I was capable of doing that made a huge difference. I felt like I was my own version of brave and it was good enough; good enough to get me away from Dad and good enough to make friends—the one thing I wanted.

Kitty, Jordan, Shea and Benji were bright and colourful and cool and all the things I would have dreamt about had I known people could be like that. They weren't like the boys who hung out on the harbour wall, and they weren't like the kids back on the estate. They were a much better fit for me. Something happened to me when I was with them. This voice started talking on my insides—a voice I hadn't heard for ages. I couldn't remember it now; it only happened when I was there. Which meant I had to see them again.

I buried my smiling face in my pillow, exhaling warm breath into the stuffing. I could still smell their fire in my hair, feel their voices laughing in my stomach. I began to laugh too.

I couldn't wait to go back to the beach that night.

I spent the whole day willing the time away, which never ever worked. I found myself checking the clock in the kitchen every fifteen minutes, striking a quarter hour off in my mind when I did and wishing a longer chunk had passed.

The further the sun moved in the sky, the closer it got to the mountains, the wilder the wings in my belly became. Eventually my body wouldn't allow me to be still any more. I must have walked from the garden, past the clock in the kitchen, to my bedroom, and back again, about twenty times. I felt like the cottage was spinning around my head.

Miraculously, I had managed to avoid Dad all day, only ever passing him occasionally in the kitchen. That was good—I knew if he looked into my eyes, if he even caught a glimpse, he would see everything: Benji, the wanderers, and my plans to see them again. It was best to stay out of his way; I didn't want him to ruin things before they had even begun. He had a knack of doing that.

But by the time the evening came, spending time with him became unavoidable.

Shuna was adamant that we all sat down together at the end of the day to eat. Every night so far she had cooked giant meals, even though there were only ever three of us, all served in the garden in matching blue and white patterned bowls. She would lay everything out on the table and we would serve ourselves—like we were at a buffet. I had never done that before Beadnell. I had never really eaten anywhere but the sofa in the front room. Oh, and the toilets at school. Food always tastes better when your nostrils are filled with the scent of Toilet Duck—said no one, ever.

I came out through the French doors, showered and fresh, with my hair washed. It felt like it had swollen to twice its original size in the heat, which wasn't ideal.

'You look well,' said Shuna as I sat down. 'Your hair is just gorgeous—so fun. Are you feeling better?' I nodded. 'Good.'

Dad sat opposite, serving himself in silence. That wasn't like him. It made me nervous. It was like he was leaving space in the air so he could focus on my movements. *Did he know already?* Was he trying to see if he could sense my betrayal in the way I reached for the bread, or uncover my plans in the way I held my knife?

'It was nice weather today,' I said.

'Aye,' said Dad. 'That's global warming for you.'

I laughed, maybe a bit too enthusiastically because he gave me the coldest look. 'Good one,' I said.

'Right,' he said, flicking his chin up.

Was the chin-flick just a casual chin-flick? Or was it an 'I-know-exactly-what-you're-up-to' chin-flick? I bloody hoped not. I couldn't have him find out now—not after last night. Before then, the people who lived in the caravan were just a mild infatuation, an itch that I really wanted to scratch—but I could have coped without doing so. Obviously, I felt differently now—and the thought that Dad could actually stop me left a really bad taste in my mouth. One that even Shuna's tuna pasta bake couldn't get rid of.

Still, I was desperate to appear as normal as possible, so I shoved heaped forkfuls of the stuff in my mouth. After a day spent in the heat and a hot shower, this turned me into a furnace. Sweat trickled down my forehead and back as I swallowed without properly chewing, washing everything down with giant gulps of juice.

'Slow down,' said Dad. 'It's not a race.'

Every spoonful felt heavy in my mouth, tasteless; every glug from my glass a missed moment on the beach. I didn't want to be there, around that table, surrounded by an old wall; I wanted to be surrounded by my new friends, picking up where we'd left off.

'How about Alnwick tomorrow?' said Dad.

'I think the market might be on,' said Shuna. 'Would you like that, Star?'

'What?' I didn't care about Alnwick, or a market. All I wanted to do was get away from them. Planning another day, thinking about tomorrow, was impossible. I only had room in my head for tonight.

'Alnwick market tomorrow,' said Dad.

'Okay,' I said. 'Great.' I wasn't really listening.

'Wonderful,' said Shuna.

I had to get away from them. *I'm going to bed.* If I didn't do it now, then I never would. *I'm tired.* It was now or never. *I need to lie down.* 'Night,' I said, standing. I wiped my mouth with my napkin and threw it on the plate in front of me. The chair fell backwards, smacking against the patio. I scrambled to pick it up. My hair fell into my face and stuck to my forehead.

'What?' said Dad.

'Bed,' I said.

'It's a bit early for you, isn't it?' he said.

'It's hot,' I said, pushing my hair out of my eyes with sweaty palms.

'Yes, it is a warm evening,' said Shuna. 'You go and rest. Make sure you take some water with you. We'll see you in the morning.'

I walked, really quickly, into the house, running when I passed the kitchen. Once I was in my bedroom, I closed the door behind me.

I stood with my back against the wood, my heart racing in

my chest. Someone knocked on the other side, and I pushed even harder against it.

‘Star?’ said Dad.

He had come to spy on me. We had known each other long enough to tell when the other was lying or not. ‘Yes?’ I said.

‘Can I have a word?’

I creaked open the door a little. ‘What?’ I said.

‘Don’t say *what* like that,’ he said. ‘I just wanted to check you’re alright.’

‘Right,’ I said. ‘I’m fine. Just tired. And hot.’

‘You’re sure?’

‘Yes.’

We stared at each other for an awkward moment. ‘Okay,’ he said, finally. ‘Well, night then.’

‘Night.’

I slammed the door shut, listening for the sound of his feet shuffling over the kitchen floor tiles and out into the garden.

Then I sprang into action.

I pulled on my white string vest, which was cut just above my bellybutton, and I threw a vintage baseball shirt over it, left open. I sprayed a sample of perfume I had found in the bathroom on the back of my neck. It was covered in dust, so I knew no one would miss it. It was called Patchouli and Jasmine. It smelt awful. Still it was better than nothing.

I shook my hair. It got bigger. *Bloody hell.* I licked my fingers and twisted sections of it around them, trying to force frizz into curls; trying to tame what was probably untameable.

And then I saw someone in the mirror. Staring at me.

I didn't recognise the person looking back. Not straight away. They had high cheekbones, sun-reddened and smooth, and really bright eyes. The sun had bleached away the stuff that needed to go and darkened the bits that needed some colour. My hair was a sandy kind of blonde around the front, and the freckles on my nose made my eyes look really blue.

I was perfectly fine, totally passable—not tragic at all.

I didn't want to stop the smile that spread across my face; didn't want to throw my hand over my mouth because I was embarrassed of it. I just stood, as still as anything, and stared.

I had never felt so ready to be seen.

I ran to the beach, taking the longer route through the village to avoid the field behind the cottage. It was like nothing else existed but getting there—or rather, getting away from Dad. As long as my evening trips could go unnoticed, I would be fine. The rest would sort itself out. That's what I told myself, anyway.

I cut through the sharp grass on the dunes, always

checking over my shoulder, just in case he was behind me. It was one thing him knowing I had escaped the cottage, but quite another him knowing the reason why. If I was caught here on the beach, I could still make up any number of excuses; once I was with them, it wouldn't be so easy.

I stopped once I knew I had cleared the tallest dune, resting my hands on my knees. A gritty feeling buzzed in my chest and scratched along my spine, twisting like vines around my legs and forearms.

Adrenaline.

I wasn't used to it. I felt as if I had a lifetime of the stuff running through me—jagged and unpredictable—changing me, making me confident and careless. I laughed a little.

I had forgotten about careless; forgotten what it felt like to be light.

My ears filled with the sound of rushing blood, crashing like the waves on the other side of the harbour wall. My heart pumped strongly. It sounded like a train passing over a railway bridge, constantly *one, two-ing,* gradually getting louder.

It wasn't long until the noise changed—turned from thudding to raised voices; laughing voices, whispering on the back of the wind, moving over the sand. Tinkling like the bells on a dream catcher and pulling me towards the black smoke that floated up into the evening, as if the wanderers were brewing *night* over their fire.

Tonight, they were in between two sailing boats which leant on their sides on the wet sand, only there because the tide was far out. In a few hours, that part of the beach would be part of the seabed again.

I walked towards them, my trainers squeezing water out of the hard sand, pressing my way between shallow pools, grooves, and worm imprints. I didn't creep. I wanted them to see me—I had risked too much to get there to waste my time on trying to disappear. For the first time I could remember, I wanted to be visible. I wanted them to notice my freckles and my eyes and my smile. I wanted to know what they thought of me. I wanted to know what *he* thought of me.

He sat on the edge of one of the slanting boats, dangling his leg over the side, leaning into the changing fire, searching the flames for something. Kitty stood beside it, while Shea and Jordan hung off the other boat.

Kitty threw things into it, just like she had the night before. The fire reacted every time she did, hissing or exhaling white smoke, reflecting onto the water like there were two fires, one above and one below.

I didn't move my eyes from Benji's face; I wanted to see his very first reaction to me. I wanted to know what he really thought.

He was handsome. Not in the way I thought boys had to be—he wasn't muscly or tall. He was lean and angular, with a kind face. He was obviously boyish; thick where he needed to be, with ears that stuck out and an unsymmetrical nose, but then he was somehow slight with long limbs; somehow girly at the same time—a mix between the two.

I approached his boat and he looked up. 'Star,' he said. He looked pleased to see me. That was a good start.

'Baby Puppy,' said Kitty, turning round. She walked towards me and pulled me forward for a hug. She smelt the same—warm and smoky. 'How are you?' she asked.

'Good,' I said.

Benji lifted me onto the side of the boat and climbed up beside me. 'There's fire on water tonight,' he said. 'You don't want to get wet.' He took a gulp from his can. He pulled out a box of cigarettes and offered me one. I shook my head. He lit one. It smelt really good. He smelt really good. He put his arm around my shoulder and pulled me in. 'It's good to see you, mate,' he said. I stayed there for a long moment before he turned his face back to the fire.

I liked that he felt comfortable enough to be so close to me. I liked that he wanted to touch me. It made my belly ache, in a really nice way.

'What are you looking at?' I asked.

‘The future,’ he said, smiling. ‘Or maybe the past—all history repeats itself sooner or later.’

I knew his answer would be clever like that. He was so unlike the boys on the estate; they were so hard and straight, and he was sort of wild and unkempt—a person who spent a lot of time outdoors. To a person who spent a lot of time indoors, that made him fascinating.

I looked at him closely, wondering if he would be the same if he came to Newcastle. Wondering if they would accept him as one of their own. He could definitely pass for a normal boy, in ways that I couldn’t. They would hate the fairy wings, of course, but I got the feeling he wouldn’t care about that.

‘Where are you from?’ I asked. I wondered if all boys were like him where he came from.

‘We’re far more interested in you, Baby Puppy,’ said Kitty. ‘Where do you come from?’

‘I’m from Newcastle,’ I said. ‘Scotswood.’ I felt embarrassed about it. It was nothing compared to this place—to the never-ending sea and the never-ending stars.

‘Do you like it there?’ Kitty asked.

‘No,’ I said.

‘Why not?’

I didn’t know where to start. I had hated every part of it ever since I moved there.

'Don't be shy,' said Benji.

'It's just not nice,' I said. 'People aren't friendly to me.'

Even saying that—even opening up that tiny amount—made me nervous. 'It's fine, though,' I said quickly. I didn't want them to think I was stupid. I wished I hadn't said anything at all.

'Is it because of the way you look?' asked Kitty.

She had found me out. She could see the real me—the freak. She could see past the tan and the freckles; the little white hairs and the Patchouli and Jasmine perfume. I knew that was a mistake.

I pulled away from Benji. I didn't want him to see me so closely anymore. I didn't want any of them to see me so closely anymore. I wanted to burrow myself into the sand like a worm, leaving nothing but a swirled cone of sand behind me.

'Because you're gorgeous,' said Kitty.

I wasn't. She was only saying it to be kind, so that I didn't feel awkward. I knew what I looked like. I knew I was girly and skinny. It wasn't good for a boy to be those things.

'Oh come on, Baby Puppy,' Kitty said. 'Look at your thick hair and your skin. I'd kill for skin like that. You're pretty, baby—those other boys are just jealous.'

Pretty. I knew I wasn't handsome. I knew I wasn't rough and ready and thick-skinned. I knew that. But *pretty*—pretty I could do. Pretty didn't seem unachievable. I didn't even know pretty was on the table. I didn't even consider it. I thought only girls could be called pretty.

But, looking around the fire at the other faces, I realised that the rules of the estate—the rigid lines outlining what was appropriate behaviour for boys and girls—didn't seem to apply. Here, masculinity and femininity were manipulated and reshaped to make new formulas—to improve old ideas and transform them into something different. And that didn't mean the wanderers were half of something and less of the other; it didn't make them any less at all. If anything, it made them more. Without rules, and with the freedom to just be, they became these beautiful creatures—completely unique and totally wild.

Suddenly, I didn't want to be a sandworm—I wanted to be just like them.

'Don't let them get you down,' said Kitty. 'They're never worth the hassle—trust me. You're perfect the way you are.'

The real me began to bubble inside again. I felt myself untangling. It was like they were the only ones that knew how to do that to me. I obviously needed to be near them all the time.

'What do you think of us?' Benji asked.

Four sets of eyes settled on me. 'I think you're all

brilliant,' I said.

'What do you know about us?' said Shea. 'What does your old man say?'

'Dad calls you wanderers,' I said. It wasn't a nice name. I suddenly felt really ashamed of him.

'I've been called worse,' said Shea.

'What do you think?' asked Benji.

'I think you're different to any other people I've ever met,' I said. 'In a really good way, I mean—it's like you learned somewhere else.'

'Learned what?' asked Benji.

'How to be *people*,' I said. I knew that sounded stupid, but I couldn't think of any other way to put it. 'Like, you must be from abroad or something?'

'We're not from here,' said Shea. 'That's for sure.' She took a drag from her cigarette, her yellow eyes unblinking; staring at me like dead eyes. 'Do you know what magic is, Jail Bait?' she asked.

It was time for another one of her shocking questions, another one of her make-Star-look-like-an-idiot moments. *Seriously, what was her problem?*

I nodded.

'Use words,' said Benji.

'Yes,' I said.

'What is it, then?' she asked.

'It's silly things,' I said. I sounded pathetic, like a kid who had just been told off.

'Like what?' she asked.

'Like making a quid disappear,' I said. It was the first stupid thing that came into my head. I had seen someone do that on Northumberland Street in town. A man with a black top hat standing at the Haymarket end. A crowd gathered round him and one of them—a little girl, I think—gave him some money and he made it disappear, then pulled it from behind her ear, like it had been there all the time.

Dad said the man was cruel, because he was taking advantage of vulnerable people, like the little girl. He said the man should be ashamed of himself. I had forgotten about that.

Shea stared at me as if she was watching my memories, as if she wanted me to say Dad's words out loud to prove that I was just like him—just as judgemental of them.

But I wasn't like Dad. I didn't think they were bad people or whatever. I didn't want to stay away from them, or pretend their caravan wasn't parked on the field. I wanted to find a way to get closer to them; that's why I was here. I was nothing like Dad.

'I suppose it can be,' Benji said. 'But there's so much more. What else?'

'I don't know,' I whispered.

My thoughts began to crisscross each other. Through the confusion, I was reminded of someone else I knew who obsessed over magic. Mam. She used to tell stories and pretend things to make our lives appear better than they were. I used to love that when I was smaller, but as I grew up, the magic turned into something else. It went from being fun to sad; flippant to really serious.

Then I remembered: all magic turned out to be lies, told by desperate people.

'It's just lies,' I said, and the words repeated again in my head in Dad's voice.

Shea smiled. Benji looked disappointed, like he had expected me to say something else. I wished I had known what; I would have said anything to not have him look at me like that again.

'That's just what I think,' I said, trying to change his face.

It didn't work.

When the morning tide came in, rushing around the little boats until they were floating again, and washing away the fire on the sand, Shea, Jordan and Kitty made their way towards the beach.

Benji stood by the side of the boat, looking into the bluish-green water, 'Are you feeling brave?' he said. I didn't reply. 'Get on my back.' He stood in front and grabbed me under the legs. 'Come on.' I gripped his shoulders and wrapped my legs around him.

He ran towards the back of the boat and jumped.

We didn't fall. Not right away. We floated in the air, suspended in time, frozen for a moment. Then we burst into a quiet, blue world.

The noises of the beach, of waves and seagulls, disappeared once we were under the surface. Replaced by nothing. Silence. I moved through a world of slow motion and blue light, over the grooved seabed where the sea had beaten and moulded the sand to mimic the surface above it.

We came up for air. He swam closer to me. 'It's lush, isn't it?' he said.

We dived again, right down to the bottom, where the water was bluer. Colder. A cluster of rocks sat under us, covered in swaying seaweed that reached up like green and brown ribbons.

We resurfaced. He dived under again and reappeared behind me. 'Do you trust me?' he said.

'Yes,' I said.

It didn't matter that we were moving further away from the

boats; it didn't matter that there was no one else around. I felt safe with him. He had already saved my life once before.

'Do you believe in me?' he said.

I thought that it was a weird question, but still I said, 'Yes.'

He grabbed my wrist and dived below the surface, pulling me down with him, faster than before.

The water pressed into my face as he led me down to colder places, through seaweed columns and sunbeams. Past clusters of rocks, where crabs scuttled sideways and anemones swayed. It was incredible, like something out of a film.

A seal dived down to greet us—an actual real-life seal! It swam around us: a round belly and limp feet bending behind it. Benji reached out his free hand and stroked it. It moved past me, brushing me with velvet fur. Benji grabbed onto it and it dragged us further.

Above, schools of fish gathered and divided in clouds of foam, weaving in and out of the morning sunlight, shimmering silver, orange and green.

We broke through the surface, and I coughed up a rush of salt water. It stung my nose. 'Bloody hell,' I said. I took a giant gulp of air, desperately trying to satisfy my need for it. 'That seal just came right up to us!' I was buzzing. I felt dizzy, moving to a different rhythm as the wind whistled in my ears.

A wave dived over my head and plunged me under. I struggled back to the surface and realised we were by the other side of the harbour, where the sea was wilder. Where the waves leapt and smashed into jagged rocks without the protection of man-made bricks and mortar. I couldn't swim on this side—I could barely keep my head above the water. Suddenly, I was reminded of *Watergate* again; suddenly I was scared of the sea and all it could do to me.

But before my legs and arms could flail in different directions, before I could sink to the bottom again, Benji came up behind me and placed his hands on my ribs, calm as anything, heaving me up and pulling me forward.

'You're alright,' he said.

He swam towards the rocks and climbed up. His clothes clung to him and I was able to see the outline of his shape, the perfection in his proportions. He was a real boy—lean where he needed to be and broad in places, each limb so well placed, so well connected.

I climbed up behind him. 'Wow!' I said. 'Wow, wow, wow. That was amazing. I thought I was going to crap myself when I saw that seal.'

'That wasn't a seal,' he said.

'I've never seen anything like that,' I said. I was shaking. Goosebumps rose along my forearms, hardening my skin.

'What do you mean, it wasn't a seal?'

'It was a selkie.'

'Don't be daft—I know a seal when I see one. I've seen those David Attenborough programmes enough times.'

He laughed. 'Selkies look exactly like seals, so how would you know?'

'Well, what exactly is a selkie?'

'They're magical creatures that look like seals, except they can shed their sealskin at night to become human.'

'Of course they are,' I said. I shook my head and began to wring the salt water out of my hair. 'You're crazy, swimming that far out—do you always do that?'

'Sometimes,' he said. 'I like a morning swim across the bay—wakes me up.'

'Right,' I said. 'Wow. If I'd have known I was going for a swim with Aquaman, I would have worn my pyjamas.'

'Your pyjamas?'

'No, I mean shorts.' *Oh well done, Star, you fool—you try to make a joke and look what happens.* 'It doesn't matter. Personal joke—I think. Sorry. Ignore me.'

'You're funny,' he said.

That made me tense up. I didn't want to be funny to him. 'No, because you wear pyjamas when you dive in the deep end of the pool,' I said, trying to sound reasonable. I only sounded more stupid. 'That's what Naseera Connolly says anyway. But she likes her stories. I wouldn't know—I dropped swimming in year eight. Sorry, I'll shut up now.'

'Don't apologise,' he said. 'I like it when you talk. You should talk more.'

I definitely wasn't going to do that.

I pursed my lips together to make sure no more stupid words could move through them.

He kept looking at me, watching with eyes that rippled with light, like the sun in the sea. 'Magic can be as easy as a morning swim with a selkie,' he said. 'Do you believe that?'

I shrugged my shoulders.

'Use words,' he said.

'Sure,' I said. 'If you want me to.'

He smiled, flashing his perfect teeth. Then he climbed up onto the harbour wall and walked back towards the water.

'Where are you going?' I said.

'To find my trident,' he said.

'Trident?'

'It's an Aquaman joke—'

'Can I see you again?'

'That's up to you,' he said.

Then he ran towards the edge and dived in, breaking through the surface without making a sound.

Eight.

Sneaking out in the dark wasn't enough. I needed mornings. I needed lazy afternoons. I needed all-of-the-time. Even thinking about him gave me this electric feeling, like I had just been plugged in. I wanted more of that feeling. I was starting to sort of need it.

There was only one problem—Dad. Dad again. Always sodding Dad. I could feel him closing in on me, even when he wasn't there. I was trying my hardest to move away, and he was moving with me. He had never been like this before; I didn't know why he had taken a sudden interest in my life—didn't he have a life of his own?

He was like this rain cloud that appeared at the breakfast table every morning and stayed with me until sundown, killing my mood with way too many questions. And I dreaded being caught out by him because I knew exactly what he would do if I was: drag me back to Newcastle, and I wasn't ready for that; I wasn't ready for it all to be over when it had only just begun.

So, my only choice was to get better at lying. I had to learn how to deceive him, to send his thoughts in completely the wrong direction so that he would leave me alone and I could spend more time with Benji and my new friends. It couldn't be that hard; I probably knew him the best out of anyone else in the world—I should have known his weaknesses.

It came to me one morning while I was on my way back from Mr Wilkinson's—an errand that was becoming increasingly hard after so many late nights. I found myself wedged up against a family in the alleyway. There were two daughters; two girls with honey-blonde hair and big horsey teeth.

'Terribly sorry,' said the dad. 'It's a bit of a tight squeeze.' He laughed and showed teeth that were just as horsey as his daughters'—probably more so, as they were closer in colour to an actual horse's teeth.

They definitely didn't come from anywhere near Beadnell. The searching looks on their faces told me they were new to the area, probably just on holiday for a few weeks. I had been around the village long enough to recognise that look.

The girls wore wetsuits, the arms tied around their waists,

colourful swimsuits on top.

'Kayaking Club is going to be so fun,' said one of them, snorting through her nose.

'I know, right?' said the other.

As they walked away from me, braying and scoffing and generally making the kinds of noises that only real posh people made, an idea began to play out in my tired head. I could pretend I had made some friends, only in the village for the summer—that bit was important because it meant our time together had a sell-by date, so I would have to see them a lot. I could pretend to be with them when I was really with Benji. There was nothing threatening about these girls; they didn't live in a caravan or wear different clothes, so Dad wouldn't care, and Kayaking Club was an actual thing—I wasn't lying about that.

I thought it was a genius idea for so early in the morning.

'I've made some friends,' I said, returning with the papers.

Shuna smiled. 'Oh, what fun,' she said.

'Who are they?' asked Dad. His eyes thinned. He looked as if he expected me to say something he didn't want to hear.

'Autumn and Amethyst Johnson,' I said. 'I'm going to the beach with them today—Kayaking Club.'

'That can't be their real names,' he said.

I had thought the same thing when I found the names in a

magazine called *Country Grandeur* in Mr Wilkinson's shop. But they kept cropping up, so I thought I would use them. And Johnson was a pretty common surname, so it wouldn't attract too much attention.

As it turned out, I took to the whole lying thing like the proverbial duck to water.

'Oh, it is,' I said, casually.

The two posh girls needed posh names. In the real world, there was no way girls like that would befriend a boy like me. Girls like that laughed at boys like me—that's if they even noticed I was there. We barely lived in the same universe. But Dad knew nothing about that.

'I thought you didn't like the beach anymore,' he said.

I wasn't quick enough to grab one of the many excuses that floated in and out of my head. I didn't want to say anything that would jeopardise my chances. So I stood in silence, staring at my reflection in his sunglasses.

'Oh, come on,' said Shuna. 'The boy probably just wants to be with friends his own age. We understand, Star. Go and have some fun.'

'Alright,' Dad said. He didn't believe me. I could tell. But that didn't matter, because Shuna did. 'Make sure you're back in time for your tea.'

After breakfast, I left the cottage through the front door. It felt exciting doing that, knowing that I was going to see him; even more than sneaking out at night because during the day there was a very real chance I would be caught.

I ran around the village, along the beach and over the dunes, thoughts of him buzzing in my head, no room for anything else.

I knew our meeting would be different. Day and night were polar opposites. I wondered if he was the same person when the sun shone, or if he would be able to see me for what I really was and would laugh at me like other boys did. The thought of that happening made me feel sick.

No. He wouldn't do that. He's my friend, I told myself.

I approached the caravan and noticed right away that something was wrong. It looked different. Wounded. Words had been written across the side in red paint—from the roof right down to the wheels, scrawled across the scratches and the windows, dripping down the side like blood.

Fairy Boys.

I banged on the door. Nobody answered. I banged again. Nothing. I pushed down the handle and pulled it towards me.

Inside smelt smoky. On the table, curls of grey grew from

a cigarette that was half ash, clinging to the side of a glass ashtray. A plant pot lay smashed on the floor.

'He's not here,' someone said. I turned to see Shea sitting on the other side of the door. 'You shouldn't be, either.'

I looked at her face; her chiselled jaw and pockmarked skin. She was angry. She frightened me, in the same way the boys on the backfield did. She was very like them.

'What happened?' I said.

She sat, open-legged, completely still, her chin lowered to her muscular chest. I wondered if she was going to lunge at me; I wondered if we were going to have a scrap. 'You've seen it, then,' she said, 'the new addition to the paintwork?'

I nodded.

'Haven't you got anything to say?' she asked. It was as if she was accusing me, like I had painted the side of the caravan and she wanted an apology.

I had seen the way girls fought on the estate. Boys were cumbersome and heavy, but girls were clever and swift. I understood them even less. A fight between boys had a structure to it; had a beginning and a very definite ending. But girls didn't play by those rules—they scratched and bit and kicked and didn't seem able to stop. They were far more terrifying.

She could have gone either way. Or maybe worse; she

could have been a mixture of both—strong and swift, or cumbersome but relentless, going and going at me until I was a quivering mess on the floor. That would be awful.

'Sorry,' I said.

'You will be,' she said, taking a drag from her cigarette. I wanted to look away from her, but I couldn't move. 'You're going to be very sorry, little Jail Bait.'

'Star,' said someone. I turned to see Benji, standing in the doorway. 'What are you doing here?'

'I wanted to see you,' I said.

'That's so good,' he said. He grabbed both of my hands and pulled me in for a hug. His body was warm and solid, like a smoothed stone left out in the sun. Suddenly, Shea couldn't hurt me. I had him for protection. 'And your dad doesn't mind?' he said.

I shook my head, forcing a smile across my clenched teeth.

'Great,' he said.

'Enjoy yourselves,' Shea said from inside the caravan. 'While you still can.'

'Oh, ignore her,' he said, pulling me away. 'She's bitter.'

He took my hand and led me into the dunes, swishing the long grass out of his way as if he weren't touching it at all, as if it were moving to let him pass. We climbed the highest dune until we reached the very top.

‘Who do you think did that to the caravan?’ he said.

I didn’t answer straight away. Shea obviously blamed me for it; I didn’t want him to blame me too. ‘I don’t know,’ I said. It was probably the boys in the village, the ones who had attacked Jordan. They had called me a fairy when they saw me.

‘What do you think about it?’ he asked.

‘I’m embarrassed,’ I said.

‘Why?’

‘Because it’s probably my fault—they think I live there too, that’s why they did it.’

He turned to look at me. A strange smile spread across his face. ‘It’s not about you, Star,’ he said.

He pursed his lips, and I saw a thought drop into his head. I could see him looking at it, moving it around, inspecting it for cracks, like he would a stone or a crystal.

I placed my hand on my pocket. Mine was still there.

‘Is that old woman your mam?’ he said.

It took me a moment to work out who he was talking about, ‘Who, Shuna?’ I said. ‘No, she’s my dad’s sister.’

‘Right.’

‘I suppose that means she’s my aunty—but I don’t call her that.’

‘Where is your mam?’

'Mam's gone,' I said, without overthinking it, without stopping myself. 'She died.'

'I'm sorry,' he said.

I nodded slowly, 'Thanks.'

'And your dad brought you here on holiday?'

'Yeah.'

'That was nice of him.'

I shrugged. He wouldn't be saying that if he knew what Dad was like; if he knew the trouble I had, and the lies I had to tell, just to see him. Or the stress Dad caused me by interfering with everything I did. Life was better in Beadnell, but only because of Benji. If Dad had it his way, he would have made me just as miserable as he was.

'Let's get out of here,' he said.

'Where to?' I said.

'Does it matter?' he said. He began to run down the side of the dune, the wings on his back flapping in the wind.

I ran after him, laughter bouncing from my stomach to my chest, sand spraying my legs in clouds under me.

If I was with him, it didn't matter at all.

A bike ride away, on two rusty old things rented from Mr Wilkinson's, we came to a valley; a basin filled with rocks and jagged edges. It looked like the mountains that towered on either side had been fighting; tearing parts off each other, and those parts lay scattered down the green mountainside.

It wasn't beautiful, not like the bay. It was stark and broken, and the stream that cut a squiggly line through the middle of it looked more mud than water.

I wondered why Benji had led us here, of all places; it would hardly win the tourist spot of the year competition. I doubted it would even make the top one hundred.

He stretched his legs out either side of his bike and allowed it to roll downhill on its own, hitting the water at the bottom at speed so mud and pebbles sprayed up the back of his shirt.

He whooped and shouted as his bike rolled along the stream. His sounds rang off the valley walls, making me aware of how big it was, and how alone we were here. That was kind of nice.

It was even nicer to watch him be so free. He held nothing back here; wetting his hair in the stream, shaking it afterwards like a dog, or a bird in a birdbath. He was so much wilder than me—so at home amongst all of this. I definitely had to try harder to be like that. Even when there was no one around I was aware of myself.

We left our bikes on the bank while we washed ourselves

further downstream, where the stream started to resemble actual water.

'Where would you like to go now?' he said.

'I don't mind,' I said. 'What else is here?'

'Well, we can go further up that way to the top of the valley, or we can go somewhere special.'

'Somewhere special?' I said.

'Yeah.'

His eyes smiled when he said it. He was really good at that—really good at smiling with other parts of his face. And it had the weirdest effect on me. It made me feel like I wasn't made of whatever people are made of, but of other stuff; air instead of skin, sand instead of bones—like if the wind blew I would go with it. I tried to get a hold of myself—I didn't want him to think I was so pathetic.

'The choice is yours,' he said.

'How far away is the *somewhere special*?' I said.

'Not far,' he said. 'We just have to follow the stream for the most part.'

'Okay,' I said. 'I'm in.'

We followed the water as it widened. It turned more into a river the deeper we went into the valley, and Benji led the way without a map. He didn't need one; he seemed to know the fallen stones almost too well. He used other things for guidance—the direction of the wind; the shadows cast by the sun; the speed of the water as it changed and grew.

The heather bushes grew taller, looking more like trees, and the broken stones turned into giant rocks, some of them big enough to climb; big enough to grip and feel the hardness of the wild against the softness of skin.

At the deepest place, where the river was white and loud and sprayed into the air until my clothes and hair were soaked, I noticed some deliberate markings on the rocks; circles and lines had been carved into them. Some had blurred over time, but most were really clear.

I ran my hands over them as we passed, allowing my fingers to fall into the grooves. To me they were just dents, but to Benji they were more than that.

Every so often, he would stop and press his palm against them, closing his eyes, waiting. It was like he could hear something above the sound of rushing water that I couldn't. And he really took the time to listen to whatever it was, and to understand what the people who lived in the valley, probably hundreds of years before, had left behind on the faces of the grey rock. It was like they were guiding him. The markings must have been directions or something, but I couldn't tell how he was reading them—they were ancient.

Soon we came to an open pool, where a waterfall tumbled

over stones like long strands of white hair over bony shoulders.

I hadn't expected to see anything like it—the rest of the valley was so plain. This place was really pretty, but not in the same way as the bay. It was nowhere near as big. It was a sort of gentler, softer version of the wild.

He climbed up onto a rock, his thick hands splayed under him, the sunlight flashing across his eyes and highlighting his glossy hair. This was his place; he looked at home, way more than he did on the beach. He could have grown here, like a twisting tree leaning over the waterfall. The calluses on his knuckles could have been part of the rocks. The shine on his hair was the same as the shine on the water. The green of his eyes was the same as the moss that covered everything. I saw him all over the place.

And being here—seeing him in his natural place—felt special, like he was showing me something that he didn't usually show people.

'Somewhere special,' I said.

'Somewhere special,' he said, opening his arms wide and tilting his head back.

'You know your way around here,' I said. I took a seat next to him.

'Reasonably,' he said.

'Is that because you're from here?' I asked.

'No,' he said. 'I wish.'

'What about those rocks,' I said. 'Can you read them?'

'Yes.'

'How?'

'By being a good listener.'

That made absolutely no sense. How could he hear something he was reading?

He stood up and pulled his shirt over his head, messing his thick hair. I felt the blood rushing to my cheeks. I looked away, too embarrassed to stare at him—too embarrassed to do the things I wanted to do, like inspect every last part of him so I could memorise it.

He looked down at the pool, moving his head from left to right. His face held the same expression as Kitty's when she lost herself in the smoke. It was as if he could see something that I couldn't.

He pulled his chest up high and dived in.

He reappeared right next to the waterfall. He sat up and stuck his head under it, allowing it to shower him clean, to grab his hair and pull it away from his face.

'Come on,' he said. 'It's not that cold.'

I looked down. I still wasn't totally comfortable with water, especially when I couldn't see the bottom. But the only way to get closer to him was to follow him.

He locked eyes with me. I felt like he was testing me, that he wanted to see if I would do it on my own, without being helped. He wanted to see if I was brave enough to do what he did.

I took a deep breath and jumped.

The water was soft. It wrapped around my shoulders like a quilt, holding me before pushing me upwards; helping me to float to the surface. I broke through and slicked my hair away from my forehead like him.

He held his hand out and helped me up onto the rock beside him. He was smiling. 'That wasn't so bad,' he said.

'No,' I said, running my hands down my face.

He sat, one leg in the pool, the waterfall spraying off his shoulders, as if he were a rock. This was his element. He was more earth than sea.

'Have you given it any more thought?' he said.

'Have I given *what* any more thought?' I said.

'Shea's question.'

'I haven't, really,' I said. I didn't feel comfortable thinking about the stuff Shea had asked me, and I still didn't have a proper answer. I was only just starting to hear my real voice again. I needed more time to understand it. 'I … I know I should be able to answer,' I said. 'I mean, I know what I feel, I know I'm not like other boys—I think I'm just complicated.'

'You know who you are, Star,' he said. 'In there.' He tapped his finger on the middle of my chest. 'But that wasn't what I was talking about. I meant Shea's other question.'

'Oh, right,' I said. I placed my hand on my forehead, hiding behind my fingers, relieved and embarrassed at the same time. 'Wait—what other question?'

'Do you know what magic is?'

I smiled, exhaling a laugh. Of course, he was joking. He was able to make a complicated situation seem light, just like the rest of his friends—arguing one minute, joking the next. I liked that about him. 'Are you really asking me?' I said.

'Well, yeah,' he said. 'I suppose I am.'

'Really?'

'Why are you so bothered?'

'I'm not, it's just—you're not serious, are you?'

'Yes.'

'Okay. Well, I think it's cute for kids,' I said, shrugging my shoulders. 'But when you get older, it goes away.' Even as the words left my mouth, I felt this unexpected twinge of sadness in my stomach. Why did that have to happen? That was just how it went, wasn't it? Everyone had to grow up sooner or later.

'Interesting,' he said.

'What?'

'That you acknowledge that there is magic, but you feel like it's gone from your life.'

'I didn't say that.'

He shrugged his shoulders. 'You pretty much did.' He slid down into the pool and disappeared, leaving me to stare at the rushing white water. Leaving me to think, which was never good.

My mind began to move in strange but familiar ways, seeping small fragments of memory into my here and now. I felt this heat rising up my chest and into my throat. Maybe the magic had gone too soon. Maybe I wasn't ready. I suppose it didn't matter now. It wasn't as if I could go back.

'We have to change that,' he said, reappearing. 'Life's too short to not believe in magic.'

I didn't say anything. I felt like he was repeating words that he had heard somewhere else to try and make me feel better. *'Life is magic'* or *'life's too short'* were the generic slogans of pretty much everything—they didn't actually mean anything. I didn't want him to talk to me like that. I wanted real things from him. And magic wasn't real.

'Can we talk about something else?' I said.

'Why?' he said.

'Because magic isn't real.'

‘You don’t know that.’

‘I do—everybody does.’

‘No, they don’t.’

‘Look, if it were real then everybody would be rich, or flying about the place, or falling in love all the time. Life isn’t like that. Bad things happen. If magic were real, then …’ I didn’t finish. I couldn’t. The heat in my throat turned into a hard lump. *If magic were real, then Mam wouldn’t have gone*, I said in my head.

‘But people *are* rich, and people *do* fall in love,’ he said.

‘Some people are,’ I said. ‘If magic were real, then don’t you think everybody would be?’

‘Everybody can be—everybody can fall in love. You’re saying it like they’re impossible things.’

‘Okay. But what about all the bad stuff you hear about on the news—what about wars and deaths and Brexit? If magic were real, then those things wouldn’t happen.’

‘I think you’re getting confused,’ he said. ‘People being cruel to each other has got nothing to do with what I’m talking about.’

He swam over to the bank and picked a dandelion clock from a thicket of grass. ‘Do you see this?’ he said. ‘Some people call these weeds. And they’re right, if that’s what they want to believe. But then, some people call them clocks to tell the time, or blow them to make wishes. The dandelion stays the same in both instances. Do you understand?'

'I don't know,' I said.

'What I'm trying to say is—it's a choice, how we view it. We can choose to believe in wishes, or we can choose to believe in nothing at all—in weeds. This dandelion doesn't look any different—it doesn't change colour or start growing another head because we think it's special. It just doesn't. But if we choose to believe in a wish we make when we blow it, who's to say it isn't going to come true?' He held the stem to his lips and blew as hard as he could. The head erupted into a hundred umbrellas, floating in and out of the light and dancing across the pool.

'Some people call these fairies,' he said, his eyes losing focus for a moment. 'Each tiny speck a fairy, struggling with the weight of a wish on its tiny wings.' He watched the seeds float away. 'So, what do you believe in, Star Stephenson from Newcastle?'

'I don't know,' I said again. The dandelion speech made my train of thought ricochet off-track.

'What do you call them?' he said.

'I've heard them called clocks before,' I said.

He smiled. 'Then that's what they are,' he said. He held up his balding stem. 'And you're running late—we should go.'

The sun was poking orange light through the skeletal trees and bushes. We must have walked for ages to get to the pool. The day was coming to an end, and thankfully, so was the conversation.

'There's a light in you, Star,' he said. 'Don't let what has happened in your past diminish it in your future. I'm not rich, nor flying about the place. This is my magic—being here at this secret pool with you. If you stop fighting against it, maybe you'll find yours.'

Mam used to talk about magic all the time. She said a day out at the supermarket was magic; or a day spent making cupcakes from a box; or a bag of hot chips on a winter's night. And I believed in her with everything that I had, and she left me. It's hard to believe in anything after something like that happens.

'Weeds or wishes,' he said, as we trekked back along the river to our bikes.

'I feel like a weed right now,' I said.

He laughed. 'You're not a weed,' he said. 'You're a star.'

We rode along the winding roads back to Beadnell, and I allowed myself to go into the caverns inside my head and use the things I knew to try and make sense of him.

I think, deep down, I knew exactly what my magic looked like—and it wasn't too dissimilar to his.

I just couldn't bring myself to admit it yet.

Nine.

The mud-stained Range Rover sat at the end of the lane, rattling like a double-decker bus, its dull green paintwork too obvious in the light of day between the redbrick walls on either side. The tell-tale smell of petrol fumes raced up to greet me as I ran away from the cottage as quickly as I could, my trainers crunching against stony ground.

The car window moved slowly down to reveal his smiling face watching me from behind the wheel, his stringy fringe falling over his sunglasses.

I looked over my shoulder to check I wasn't being followed or watched from the other side of the garden wall. Dad did that sometimes.

He was playing a very dangerous game coming to meet me so close to home. As if meeting in daylight wasn't enough of a risk.

My heart thudded in my chest as I ran towards the car and pulled open the door. 'Drive,' I said, throwing myself inside. 'He'll kill me if he sees me.'

He pressed his foot down on the accelerator and we sped off, dust flying up into the air behind us. 'I thought you said he didn't mind,' he said.

'He doesn't know,' I said. I was laughing—my natural reaction to adrenaline, it seemed. Blood pumped into my cheeks, and my limbs felt light as string. I couldn't control my belly from jumping up and down. Vibrating like the engine. 'Sorry,' I said, wiping my mouth with the back of my hand.

I could tell he didn't find it as funny; he shrank in his seat beside me, deflating like a helium balloon after a kid's birthday party. 'It doesn't matter,' he said. 'I just thought—you're getting along better with him here though, right?'

The question seemed odd, like he was concerned about Dad. Concerned about Dad and me. 'Not really,' I said. I hadn't given it a thought; I didn't think it mattered. He clearly did.

'That's a shame,' he said. 'You should be kinder to him—he's been kind to you.'

It was my turn to shrink, my turn to feel inadequate. I felt like he was trying to make me feel bad for something I didn't know I had done. Maybe I should have been kinder to him. I didn't see how that was his problem, though. 'Sorry,' I said again.

'Don't be,' he said, 'just think about it. But not today—today we're going to have fun.'

And just like that, the air between us cleared and he was light again—the sun, chasing away the dark.

We headed inland, past villages smaller than Beadnell—some of them only a handful of houses, a railway crossing, sometimes a school. We headed towards the Cheviot Hills—giants lying on their sides, covered in black moss. I didn't feel as drawn to them as to the sea. I didn't feel as safe with giants.

My ears popped as we drove higher, climbing beyond farming fields and villages up to flat plains where tarmac roads cracked and rose and turned to dust.

It was quiet, just like the sea, but not as magical. Eerie. Pensive silence; like the kind that came before a storm.

Benji turned the car off the road and we rolled to a stop. He jumped out and walked around the car to open my door.

Moss-covered stones littered the place like landmines. The silence was too obvious. There was no one around, only hills and sky.

And us. Picking our way through it all.

He seemed uneasy up here, always looking over his

shoulder, like I did when I ran from Shuna's cottage. I wondered if he was running from something too.

'What do you believe in?' he asked me.

'What do you mean?' I said.

'Well, what's important to you—what makes you feel angry, or happy or sad?'

I knew the answer. I didn't have to give it much thought at all. I could pinpoint all of those feelings on one thing, on one person. Mam. She made me feel all of those things. She was always on my mind, right there at the top of everything. Still. Even after she had been gone for over two years, when I should have found a way to move on. Everything I felt was because of her.

'The sun makes me happy, I think,' I said. I still didn't know if I was ready to talk about her. 'Being outside.'

'That's good,' he said. 'What else?'

I didn't want to say what was on my mind. I didn't want him to think a certain way about me.

'I'm not scared,' he said, shaking his head. 'You can tell me what's on your mind—what makes you sad?'

I took a deep breath. 'I'm sad that me mam died,' I said.

Still, two years on, it didn't feel real. Most of the time, in the beginning, I felt like she was on holiday; somewhere far, like Australia or something. The thought that she was really gone forever was too much for me to cope with, I suppose.

Then a moment would come when it would all hit me at once. A song would come on the radio, sung in her voice; a memory would play in my head like a reel of film, and I would remember she was gone. I would shake my head and scrunch my eyebrows and clap my hand to my mouth. I would feel a dark space opening up inside of me, and I would feel myself slowly falling into it, hitting every rough edge on my way down, until I hit the ground.

Sometimes it took days to get back up from there; to be able to see the light of day without feeling like a fraud.

'How did she die?' he said.

No one had asked me that question before. No one wanted to talk about *how*. 'They called it a chemical imbalance,' I said.

'Who did?'

'Well, everyone—doctors and teachers and the social worker that came round to the house every Wednesday after school.'

'What did they say?'

'They kept talking about trauma and stress and how I was very young to lose a parent. As if I didn't know that. They told me not to blame her, and not to blame myself. They were pretty clear about that—I was allowed to blame the chemical imbalance, though. Even before I knew what it was.'

'What is it?'

I didn't answer straight away. No one had ever explained it to me; I was never brave enough to ask either. I had ended up giving it my own explanation—making up something that sort of made sense to me.

'You don't have to talk about it if you don't want to,' he said. 'I'm only asking because I want to know you better.'

I wanted that too. And I wanted her to be a part of my friendship with him. I wanted to see her on the beach, or here on the hillside. If I spoke about her, maybe that would happen. She would have loved it here.

'Well, she was depressed,' I said. 'That makes it sound like she was sad all the time. She wasn't. Everybody loved her. She was always laughing, always seeing the joke quicker than anyone else, like she had her own way of thinking. That's what it is, I think—a different way of thinking.

'God, she really made you feel special. But then she'd have these dark days. She'd become erratic—really talkative and quick, like she couldn't focus on anything for too long. I couldn't keep up with her. It was like she had dived underwater and she was trying to swim to the top as fast as she could and that was all that mattered.' My words were spilling over the edges of my lips, as if there was no room for them inside of me anymore, as if they all had to come out.

'Before she died, she had been more like that than not. I remember her being really dark all the time and arguing with Dad a lot. It was horrible, really.

'And then one day at school I was called in to the headteacher's office and I knew exactly why. I sort of always knew she would do it, which made it worse because I should have been able to stop her.

'Sometimes I see her and it's so real. Sometimes I talk to her and she answers me, like she's really there.

'Anyway, that's what makes me sad,' I said, wiping my nose with the back of my hand, 'and scared, I suppose, too. I get scared her darkness will become mine.'

'It won't,' he said. 'You are not to blame. You're so brave, Star.'

'I'm not,' I said. I knew what bravery looked like.

'You are. You're so full of love. You can't see it, but everybody else does. You keep pushing forward—you keep going to people.'

He pulled my head in towards his and pressed our foreheads together. His was warmer than mine. Being that close to him, close enough to feel his heat and smell his breath, calmed me down; it helped ease the feelings I had just dug up and dropped on the ground.

I knew the pain would never go away altogether. But in that moment, it didn't feel as heavy to carry.

'I know Dad worries,' I said. 'I know he thinks I'm more like her than him.'

'And are you?' he said.

'Yes,' I said. 'Dad says she was a dreamer, and I'm the same.'

'He cares about you.'

'He doesn't want me to see you,' I said. 'He doesn't want me to see any of you.'

'He's scared,' said Benji. 'He's trying to protect you. He doesn't know us.'

'But I don't need protecting from you.'

He looked down, and I felt part of him pull away from me.

I suddenly realised I had been talking about myself for ages. 'What about you?' I said. 'What makes you sad?'

'Nothing, really,' he said. 'I don't allow myself to be sad.'

'You make it sound so easy.'

'I don't have anything to be that sad about,' he said. 'I think it's good to talk about things. Get them off your chest. I think it's sad when people can't do that. When friends or families don't do that.'

I nodded slowly. That was a really good answer. I wished I had thought of something like that.

'I … I want to tell you something,' he said. He looked a bit agitated again, checking over both shoulders. 'But you can't tell anyone. You have to promise.'

'Okay,' I said.

'I'm not like other boys,' he said. 'I'm different.'

'I know that,' I said.

'You do?'

'Of course I do—you're nothing like the boys on the estate. You're so much gentler, and I think that's really, really brilliant.'

'Right,' he said. 'Yeah. Well—thanks.'

'I mean it,' I said. I was starting to get that really nice feeling in my belly again—the gentle, achy feeling.

'Good,' he said. 'I think you're really brilliant too.'

The achy feeling got bigger really quickly. It expanded like I had a hot air balloon inside of me. I felt a little bit dizzy. Maybe it was the altitude.

'Will you fly with me?' he said.

'What?' I said.

'Fly with me.'

He stretched his arms out either side and began to run, as if he had real wings that could carry him up through the clouds into the pale sky.

I ran after him, the wind pulling my hair away from my

face. I stretched my arms out too, as wide as I could, and allowed the achy feeling to lift me up.

I was definitely lighter—I wouldn't have been able to fly with him had I not been.

That night, my dreams were strange.

The mountains came to life, standing up from their sleeping places and shaking away the heather and moss that grew along their arms, down their sides and in between their eyes. They stomped towards the sea, returning to their home after a sleep that had lasted for a thousand years. Crunching up the countryside, flattening villages and fields.

Horses with fish tails and mermaids with greasy hair—thick with oil—and crooked teeth met them at the water's edge. They tried to lure me towards the water and drown me in a black sea, full of death and noise. They grabbed at me and held me down onto the seabed. Their faces were angry and harsh—like the boys on the estate. Like Shea.

'You've shown him too much,' she said, her yellow eyes alive with fire—not usual fire, not throbbing and heavy, but thin, clever and sly, like the reflection of fire on water.

'I haven't shown him anything,' said Benji. 'He's seen it himself. He's different.'

'He's just like the rest of them. Open your eyes. Do you know what kind of danger you've put us in?'

'I haven't shown him anything.'

Their voices were as real as if they were standing next to me; as if they were outside my open window or beside my bed.

'We were called here to grant a wish,' said Shea, 'not expose ourselves to danger. You've gone about this all wrong. We have to go.'

'The wish hasn't been granted,' said Benji. He was shaking. I hadn't seen him like that.

'Not all wishes are granted,' said Shea. 'Not all wishes matter.'

'His do,' he said. 'He matters.'

'Then why do you care?' said Shea. 'It's not even his wish.'

Ten.

Dad sat at the table in the garden, moving his eyes over the morning paper far too quickly to actually read anything, his foot steadily tapping off the patio. 'You seem to be spending a lot of time with those girls,' he said. 'Why don't you bring them over?'

Girls—what girls? Oh right, yeah. My fake friends. 'They won't come,' I said. 'I've already asked.'

'Are we not good enough for them?'

'No. We just prefer the beach and stuff—Kayaking Club and all that.'

'What's with this new kayak obsession—are you planning on joining the Olympic team, like?'

He was angry. He got sarcastic when he was angry. I hadn't heard him like that for a while.

I felt my shoulders rise up to my ears. There was more to his questions than him wanting to meet two made-up girls with made-up names. I knew it. He was trying to trip me up; trying to get the truth out of me. This awful feeling, like freezing water, rushed down the sides of my body. I suddenly didn't want to be near him. Everything was going great; I didn't want him to ruin it.

My initial reaction was, as always, to run; to go back indoors and avoid him for the rest of the day—the rest of the summer, if I could. But Benji had told me I had to be strong. Use my voice. *Always use words*—that's what he said.

It was time to put that into practice.

'No,' I said.

He returned to his newspaper, pretending to read as if nothing had been said. As if he didn't want to acknowledge the change in me. *Had it really worked?* 'That caravan's still there,' he said. 'The old gadgie in the shop said he hoped they'd be gone by now. Nobody wants people like that around.'

'Why do you care?' I said, gaining confidence with every word that spat out of me. 'They're not bothering you.'

'What?'

'Well, what have they done to you that's so bad?' I stared right into his dark, lifeless eyes, determined not to move.

I hadn't looked at him for such a long time; not that closely, anyway. I didn't recognise the person in front of me. Not one bit of him belonged to my dad, the one who used to talk to me; the one who used to stand on the top step waiting for me to return home from school; the one who used to take me up to the top road and let me drive his car. That dad was gone. Whoever was sitting at the table with me now may have been wearing his clothes, may have even shared his eyes, but that was where the similarities ended.

'They're not good people,' he said. 'I've told you.'

'You don't know anything about them.' I was pushing; pushing a tonne weight; pushing me; pushing him. *Always words*. 'Maybe you should mind your own business and leave them alone.'

He snapped his paper shut and slammed it down on the table. 'You're hiding something,' he said. 'You're a terrible liar, Star. Always have been.'

I had said too much. Pushed too far. As soon as the words left my mouth, I wanted them back. I knew he would read more into them. I may as well have told him everything. I was such an idiot.

'I'm not,' I lied.

'If I find out this has got anything to do with *them*,' he began.

You'll what? I thought. I didn't dare say it. I wasn't brave enough to push any further, even if that's what Benji would have done. I just stared at the half-eaten bacon sandwich on the plate in front of me; the tasteless, chewy, heavy sandwich that suddenly felt like a brick in my stomach. 'It hasn't. Alright?' I said.

'I mean it, Star,' he said. 'We'll be out of here quicker than crap off a shovel. You stay away from that caravan.'

It was my own fault, really. I had allowed myself to get too comfortable. By getting swept up in all of these new things, I had forgotten about the old ones. I had deluded myself into thinking that I was actually free to do what I liked, and not, in fact, telling lies to sneak away from the one person who controlled everything I did. That morning over breakfast, Dad had given me a short, sharp dose of reality. And it had brought me crashing back down to earth from whatever number cloud I had been floating on for the past couple of weeks.

I was seriously sick of him.

I couldn't see why he hated my friends so much. Yeah, they were different; yeah, they weren't his type of people. But they weren't harming him. From where I was standing, they weren't bothering him in any way. He seemed to be massively overreacting, and to something that didn't actually exist.

But that didn't matter. Dad had thrown down the gauntlet, and I couldn't just ignore it. If he caught me with Benji, I would be carted off back to Newcastle, to the way things were before.

And, even if he didn't, I would have to go back soon anyway. So, either way, he was going to ruin everything.

The thought of the estate, of stuffing myself back into a shoebox when I had experienced life here, seemed impossible. The goldfish couldn't go back into the bowl after it had been freed; it would die. I felt like I would do the same. I felt hopeless. Cornered. And, for the first time since *Watergate*, I started to feel really sad again.

The new colours began to fade. A dark cloud moved up my spine and rounded over my head, covering my eyes in grey, just like it did with Mam. I understood her more every time that happened.

All it took was one morning—one morning without Benji; one morning of just thinking about what came next—for me to return to the darkness. One bloody morning. *How was I supposed to get through the rest of my life?*

The cloud began to push against my sides until I could only move inwards; fall deeper into myself. I hated this. Come on; there had to be a way to make it work—to show Dad how important and rare it was for someone like me to find real, like-minded friends. Surely he knew that? I mean, it wasn't as if the kids on the estate were queuing down the garden path, begging me to come out with them. The only person I spoke to at home was Naseera, and she only ever shouted over the back fence when she was bored.

If he really did know that I had made friends with the people from the caravan, then he should have also known how important they were to me. Surely he could see that I needed them? I needed this place.

Maybe he did. Maybe he just didn't care.

I was spiralling out of control. Hitting every rough edge as I made my way down the black hole again. Falling towards an unknown target, or maybe no target at all—just nothing, trapped in purgatory.

I needed to lie down. My bed was calling me again. *Come on, Star—get a grip*. I didn't want to be this person. *Think, you idiot*. I was running from the boys on the backfield; I was falling off the harbour wall again, suspended in the air, about to plunge into nothingness. They were laughing; they were always laughing. I wasn't this person. *Come on*. I wasn't this person.

I wasn't her.

'Is everything okay?' asked a voice. I looked up. It was

Shuna, smiling down at me with happy eyes.

'Yes,' I said. I tried to smile too. It was a real effort.

'Are you sure, Star? You look a bit peaky. Let me get us some fresh lemonade.' She swept into the kitchen, reappearing with two tall glasses. 'I like to add lavender honey to my lemonade,' she said. 'It's magic stuff. Now, what's going on?'

I took the glass and sipped. The lemonade exploded in my mouth in a perfect mix of sweet and sour. I felt myself slowly returning—maybe lavender honey *was* magic stuff.

'How is it?' she asked.

'Nice,' I said.

She gave me two thumbs up, scrunching up her face like she was really pleased; pleased that her lemonade was a success, pleased that I was enjoying it—or just pleased for the sake of being pleased. Shuna seemed to have the happiness thing down. I never saw her without a smile in her eyes, not really. Maybe she could help me be like that. I felt like I could speak to her and, to be honest, I had to speak to someone. My thoughts were too heavy to carry on my own. 'I don't know what to do,' I began. 'Well, maybe I do. I mean, Shuna …' I mumbled, 'can I ask you something?'

'Anything, my dear boy,' she said.

'I need some advice,' I began. 'I've made some friends and I don't think Dad would be happy with them.'

‘I know,’ she said.

‘What?’

‘I know you’ve made friends with the people from the caravan,’ she said. ‘I think the whole village does. You’re not as discreet as you think you are, Star.’

‘Does he know?’ I suddenly felt dizzy and disorientated, like my ears were stuffed with cotton wool. He couldn’t know for sure; he would have said something.

‘I don’t think so,’ she said. ‘He’s actually bought your Kayaking Club story, believe it or not. But the village is small, and people like to talk.’

‘He definitely hasn’t said anything, though?’

‘No, Star, he hasn’t. But sooner or later he’s going to find out.’

‘You won’t tell him?’

‘It isn’t my place to tell,’ said Shuna.

‘Okay,’ I said. ‘Thank you.’ I knew I could trust her.

The whole ‘being discreet’ thing I could definitely get better at, and now I knew Dad might hear some gossip about me in the village, I could have a story ready to throw back at him—maybe something about one of the kayaking girls knowing someone from the caravan so our group had mixed a little bit. *What were their names again?*

I exhaled a sigh of relief. Okay, so that was one thing

sorted. Good.

Now it was on to the bigger problem—a problem I had never thought about before. Time. Summer had to come to an end, and even if Dad didn't know about Benji now, he wouldn't exactly be inviting him round to our house for Christmas dinner. I needed to find a way of keeping Benji in my life but without Dad knowing anything about him; of turning a summer with him into, well, more than that.

Basically, I had to find a way to change the inevitable.

'Shuna,' I began, 'what happens next, like, when I go home?'

'Well,' she said, 'you'll go back to normality.'

Normality. There was no such thing. It seemed everybody had their own version of it.

For Dad, normality was black and white stripes, football on a Saturday, and chips and curry sauce for tea. For the kids on the estate, it was hanging about by the chippy on the top road, drinking cider and asking passers-by to buy them cigarettes. For the wanderers, it was moving from place to place, living by their own rules, sleeping under the stars. Where did I fit in amongst all of that?

In Newcastle, the only constant in my life was loneliness. But here in Beadnell, I was so many things; I was pretty and funny and dangerous. I mattered. I had to find a way to still matter in a place that didn't accept me. That seemed impossible. My old 'normality' didn't exist, and my new one couldn't. For me, it wasn't a question of going back. I had to find a way to move forward.

'And that's it,' I began, 'it's just over?'

'It's never over,' said Shuna. 'The memories will always be with you.'

Memories. I didn't want memories. I wanted real things. I had spent the last two years living off memories, off wind and shadows. They were no substitute for what was real. 'But what if I want more than that?' I said.

'Then you'll have to come back,' she said. 'Make more. You're always welcome.'

Wait a minute—was I hearing right? I could come back whenever I liked and, more importantly, come back and see *him* whenever I liked? Yes, that's exactly how we could make it work—weekends and bank holidays and end-of-term breaks. *Brilliant.* I could end up spending nearly half the year here. That would be amazing. Every Friday, right after school, I could jump on the train. He could pick me up from Berwick in the car. Kitty wouldn't mind. I would pretend I was staying at Shuna's to keep Dad happy, but I would really be under the stars with Benji. Then, before we knew it, it would be summer all over again. *Perfect.*

'This changes things,' I said aloud without meaning to.

I jumped up from the table and ran inside, passing Dad in the hallway. 'Where are you going?' he asked me.

'Out,' I shouted.

'But what about Alnwick—'

'Sorry,' I called over my shoulder. I didn't have time to talk to him; I had to tell Benji what our future looked like.

'I'm sick and tired of this,' I heard him say to Shuna.

He sat on the harbour wall, swinging his legs over the edge, where the sand met the water. I wondered if he ever slept. I woke up because I had to, so it didn't look like I was sneaking out of the house every night. Appearing at the breakfast table was the worst part of my day. I found it exhausting at the best of times. He didn't have that problem; he could have snoozed until midday if he'd wanted to.

'Star,' he said as I ran towards him along the water's edge.

He jumped down and moved towards me, pulling me in for a hug like he always did.

'I can come here when I want,' I said.

'What?'

'Here—I can come here whenever I want, like weekends and stuff.'

'That's good,' he said.

His face didn't change. He didn't look up from the sand. *That's good?* It was better than good. It was incredible; fantastic; life-changing—it was a year or so of weekends and holidays, just like the summer; every day spent in the sea or on the beach, every night spent sitting under the stars together. It was the continuation of this weird magic thing we had, until next summer came and we could do it all again. It was our future. It was everything. *Good* didn't come anywhere near it. 'You don't seem to be too happy,' I said.

'Summer will be over before we know it,' he said.

'Yes, but, you're not listening—I'll probably be back the first weekend of term.'

'It doesn't matter.'

'Why not?'

'Because I won't be here.'

I clapped my hand to my forehead to ease the sudden headache that shot into my temples. 'Sorry?' I said. My insides all twisted around, like my organs were separating and rearranging themselves; my stomach somewhere near my knees and my heart firmly wedged into my throat. I felt embarrassed that I couldn't control the way my body reacted. Couldn't control how I felt in the way that he could. 'What do you mean?' I asked. My voice sounded so girly and stupid.

'You know what I mean,' he said. 'We don't stay in one place. We're *wanderers*, as your dad says.'

My temples throbbed again, harder than before. I could barely look up at him. Barely keep my eyes open. 'But, you don't go far,' I said. 'You'll be near enough to come back at weekends.' *How far could an old Range Rover and a tiny caravan go?*

'We go where we need to,' he said.

'What does that mean?' I asked.

'Exactly that—we don't stay around here.'

'But you don't go that far.'

'We go far enough.'

I could tell he was sad about it. I could tell he didn't mean to make me feel like he didn't care. I could tell he didn't mean to make me feel like he was stamping all over my stomach and then dropkicking it into the sea.

But it was like he didn't even want to try. I could see it all over his face. There was no way to avoid the end of summer. No way to soften the blow. No weekends and holidays to take the edge off. Just the time we had left. Weeks. Barely that.

'Okay,' I said. 'So, you don't even want to try?'

'It's not as simple as that, Star,' he said. 'We spend winter in other places. Further south. I can't just get here for weekends and go back. And where am I going to stay—with that old lady? I'm sure her invitation extends to the weird wanderer boy.'

'It will. Shuna's nice.'

'Yeah, I'm sure she is. Until she's not.'

There was no changing him. I felt like there was a bigger reason why he couldn't come back to Beadnell; one he wasn't prepared to talk to me about. Maybe it was because he was about to go somewhere far away. And maybe there was more to it than that—I got a feeling there might have been, but what did it matter? When summer ended, I would never see him again.

'Don't think about that now,' he said, grabbing my hand. 'We still have today.'

A butterfly appeared. Its wings were black, red and white. It circled his head, searching for somewhere to land. It finally landed on his hand.

'Look,' he said, 'Have you ever seen one like this?'

'I don't know,' I said. I barely looked at it. I didn't want to talk about butterflies.

'A monarch,' he said, holding it up. 'People call these wanderers, you know, because they travel so far from home.' It flapped its wings two or three times and launched into the morning. He watched it flitter away, a gentle smile spreading across his face, creating grooves down either cheek. 'People say that they can't face strong winds,' he said. 'They're too light, so they just float and allow themselves to drift to wherever they land. I think, sometimes, people get it wrong. I think everyone knows exactly where they want to go. Just some have to work a little bit harder to get there.'

I didn't go back to the cottage for tea like I usually did. I didn't care. I would make my excuses later. I didn't want to waste a second. Time was too precious. The thought that it could all be over so soon scared me more than anything else did. Benji had given me all of the things I had wanted, all of the things a summer was supposed to be, and before I knew it he would be gone.

It felt worse than if I had never met him at all, if I had just stayed in my bedroom, under the covers, for the whole summer.

The reasonable voice inside my head, the one I had ignored for weeks, jumped back in and shouted so loudly I had to clap my hand over my head again.

It said—*I told you so.*

Eleven.

The beach was quieter that night. Our firelight was like a single candle in the dark. Every time someone spoke, their words mixed with the wind, the crackling fire, the sea, until they became much more than just one voice. They became everything.

They *were* everything—everything to me, anyway. I couldn't imagine life without my friends. I couldn't imagine life without this.

Shea had already left Beadnell, and no one wanted to explain why—Jordan least of all. He sat on his own with his back to the rest of us, drinking can after can of beer and staring out to sea like a dog that had lost its owner. Every so often, he would look over his shoulder at me and roll his eyes. He looked agitated, like he wanted to speak to the others but couldn't with me there.

'What's wrong with him?' I asked Benji.

'Nothing,' he said. 'He's fine.'

He clearly wasn't. Jordan blamed me for something. I could feel his anger in every sharp turn of his head. If there was one thing I had learned about them, it was that their actions spoke much louder than their words.

I felt totally awkward sitting there with Benji on one side and Kitty on the other, none of us really talking. Shea's absence was too noticeable and I, for the first time all summer, felt unwelcome, which made everything that had happened that day seem totally worse.

'Should I talk to him?' I asked.

'No,' said Benji. 'Honestly, he's fine. Don't worry about it.'

Kitty shuffled closer and rested her head on my shoulder. 'How are you, Baby Puppy?' she asked.

'I'm okay,' I said. 'How are you?'

'Tired today,' she said. Her voice sounded different. Lighter. Like she was fading away.

I had this horrible feeling that they were moving on much sooner than I expected. Maybe I didn't have days at all. Maybe I only had tonight.

Was the dream I had about the argument outside of my

bedroom window real—had Shea gone because Benji had shown me too much?

But shown me too much of what?

Knowing Shea, she wouldn't just storm off and leave her friends for anything—and she had never shied away from a confrontation with me before. Most of the time she seemed to quite enjoy it. Running away just didn't seem like something she would do, unless something really serious had happened.

'Where has she gone?' I said.

'Don't worry about her,' Benji said. 'She's a big girl—she can look after herself.'

This was just so awkward, like there was a giant, pink elephant sitting on the side of the dune and nobody was allowed to talk about it.

'I'll miss you all,' I said. I had to say something.

'Everyone needs to lighten up,' said Benji. 'Honestly—everything is fine.'

'You're right,' said Kitty, scratching her fingers through her messy hair. 'Someone pass me my bag.'

I reached over for the small leather rucksack covered in metal studs that lay on its side by the fire. I passed it to her. She flipped over the top and rummaged around inside. She pulled out a box of cigarettes and lit one. 'Baby Puppy,' she said, 'a dear old friend of mine used to say that there was no situation in the world that couldn't be made better with a little bit of drag.' She pulled out a smaller makeup bag. 'I've been dying to attack those eyelashes with my magic mascara wand. Come here.'

'Drag?' I said. 'Ah no, I can't.'

'Come on, you'll look gorgeous once I'm finished. Trust me.'

'Go on,' said Benji, rubbing the back of my neck.

The voice of Dad jumped into my head. I knew what he would say—*Lads don't wear makeup*. It made me want to do it more. I was so tired of him telling me what to do. This was all his fault.

I tilted my head back and closed my eyes. Kitty came closer. So did the smell of almond oil and smoke. She began to rub and flick and smudge my eyes with her fingers. She lined my eyes with black pencil and brushed mascara on my eyelashes and eyebrows. I couldn't deny it felt nice being touched like that.

'Smile,' she said. She then spread something across my lips, dabbing it with her fingers. 'Oh, she's gorgeous—here, have a look.'

I opened my eyes, 'Wow,' I said, grabbing the mirror.

I looked good. But like, really, really good. My eyes looked so much better with makeup around them, like they were always supposed to look like that. The white bits looked really white and, even in the orange firelight, my irises looked bluer. My eyelashes were almost double the length, and the bags under my eyes, gained from weeks of no sleep, had gone. I looked better than any girl I had seen.

There had been many times in my life when I had felt detached from who I knew I really was. Like in P.E. class, or when I was watching the other boys on the estate. I would feel myself slipping away. My body would go through the motions but the other me—the real me—would be off, running through the rooms in my head, searching for a happy place to rest for a while.

This was the happy place. That's the only way to describe how I felt. It was like my head and my body and the moving bits inside of me were all in alignment; were all part of the same person—the person in the mirror.

I looked just like one of them.

'You're really good at makeup,' I said to Kitty.

'Thanks,' she said. 'It comes from years of watching and wishing.'

'Well, it paid off,' I said. I was, weirdly, more confident as this person.

'You have no idea,' she said. 'You're next, our Benji—get over here.' She sat beside him and placed her hand under his chin, her fingers splayed and delicate.

'Come and do me,' he said to her.

'You wish,' she said.

She tilted his head back and began to work, applying small amounts of eyeliner and shadow and gradually building them into something beautiful, like an artist.

'When I was little, I used to dream of growing up to wear makeup just like my mother,' she said. 'I want to tell you something, Star.' She continued to work on her masterpiece, not looking at me but talking directly to me.

'My path into womanhood was a little different,' she said. 'I was born knowing exactly who I was, and also knowing that my body was wrong. I think, deep down, we're all born knowing exactly who we are—it's other people who seem to mess things up for us. *Look up*.' She pointed her finger to the sky and lifted Benji's chin with her other hand. '*Right, don't blink*. It took me a while to find the courage to be the person I knew I was, but when I did, my whole world changed. So, what I'm saying to you is—be *you*, Star. Whatever you feel like that is.'

I let her words sink through my skin. I felt this connection to her. I had felt it since the first day I looked into her eyes through Mr Wilkinson's shop window. It was like she could see me on the inside. She could see who I really was. She could see the alignment that happened when I looked at my face in the mirror. She recognised it because she had been there too, once.

'I think I'm like you,' I said. 'I'm not like other boys. I'm not like Benji—I look at him and definitely see a boy, even with the fairy wings.' Benji laughed. I carried on. 'I'm not like that. I don't feel masculine. It's like I'm made out of water or something—I'm never what I think a boy should be.'

She looked at me, nodding. 'It's good that you feel all of those things, Star,' she said. 'Don't be afraid of them.'

'But I *am* a boy,' I said.

'And that doesn't have to mean what you think it means,' she said. 'Maybe you're masculine, maybe you're feminine, and maybe you're non-binary, or changeable. That's okay too. All of it is right if it feels right.'

'What's non-binary?' I said. I had never heard that before.

'It means you don't play by their rules,' she said, throwing her chin up in the air. 'And nor should you.'

I smiled at her little performance. 'I can't be like this at home,' I said. 'The other boys would tear me to bits—I'm different enough without this. I don't know what I'm going to do.' I was spurting out whatever was in my head; talking to anybody and nobody at the same time.

'Oh, sod them,' she said. 'Don't look at those other boys

and feel sorry that you're not like them—feel sorry for them that they're not like you, and they have to live their lives constrained by their own tiny ideas. You only get one life, Star. Do you want to spend it happy or unhappy?'

'Happy,' I said.

She laughed, as if the question didn't need an answer. Rhetorical, I think it's called. 'Put on makeup,' she said, 'wear the sparkly wings. It's your choice. For me, being feminine is my way of saying to the world—this is who I am, and this is how I expect to be treated.'

'Like a lady,' said Benji.

'Et voilà!' said Kitty, clicking her fingers.

I smiled. 'Thank you,' I said.

'Oh, there's nothing to thank me for,' she said. 'You'll do all the work, Star. Just know that whatever you feel inside is right. Focus on that, and when life gets a little complicated, or the voices of those other lads drown out your own, you'll still be able to feel who you are.'

'Oh, she's good,' said Benji.

'I feel like his chuffing fairy godmother,' she said. 'You shall go to the ball, Star.' She flicked her mascara wand.

All summer long, I had been trying to work out what their secret was, and it turned out to be really simple—put on the makeup; wear the wings. That was it. Just do *you*.

I was allowed to like myself. I was allowed to be different to the other kids on the estate. I was original. One of a kind, just like Naseera said. And that was good enough.

Benji turned to me. He was even better with makeup on, if that was possible. His almond-shaped eyes suited dark eyeliner so much. They looked like a tiger's eyes or something; I could feel my heart racing in my chest when he looked at me because I knew it wasn't only Kitty sitting by the fire; he had heard every word I said too. He had heard the real me.

'Aw, look at you both,' said Kitty. 'You're both gorgeous.'

'Don't go,' I said. It came from my stomach instead of my throat, like my insides were talking. I wanted that, of course, maybe more than I could admit, but I didn't mean to say it.

Kitty reached forward and rubbed my earlobe between her thumb and forefinger. 'We have to,' she said.

'But I need you.'

She looked at Benji. He stood up and held out his hand. 'Come on,' he said. He pulled me up from the sand and led me away from the dunes, towards the sea.

The moon shone a perfect pathway of light towards us, as if we could just walk over water to the giant white orb in the sky, to a place where we didn't have to worry about summer coming to an end because there were no summers on the moon. I would have gone there with him. I would have gone anywhere.

'You look cute,' he said. Our hands were still interlocked. His was so warm and rigid; a proper boy's hand. He stood in front of me so we were facing. 'Close your eyes.'

I did.

His hand found the back of my head and, pulling me forward, he pressed our foreheads together.

I felt really strange, like I was moving into him, melting through his skin until we were sharing a body. We were one and the same; two parts coming together to make a whole. My hands were his hands. My heart was his heart.

And I was floating above the bay, through black space, past stars and clouds of dust. And everything was alive; the grass and the wind and the sea all had voices of their own. This was his magic; this was our magic.

'This is who you are,' he whispered in my ear. 'This is the world.'

I felt myself laughing. I couldn't stop. Being that close to someone, being that close to him, was out-of-this-world amazing. Fireworks exploded in my belly. I could hear his blood in his veins.

'You can see everything, can't you?' he said.

'Yes.'

'I knew it,' he said. 'I knew it from the moment I looked at you. What am I?' he asked.

My mouth hung open. 'What do you mean?' I said.

'Think about it,' he whispered. 'What am I?'

'You're …' I began, 'you're my friend.'

'No.'

'My best friend,' I said quickly.

He shook his head. His face was as wild as the fire; his eyes full of movement, his lips parted, his nostrils flaring. He was trying to tell me something without using words, as if I had to be the one to say it.

'That's enough,' said an angry voice. Jordan was standing beside us. 'What do you think you're doing?' he said.

The sky was lighter. I felt confused, disorientated, like I had just woken up.

'Benji,' Kitty began, 'you shouldn't—'

'I haven't done anything wrong,' he said. He looked like a kid that had just been caught. 'He's my friend.'

'I know,' said Kitty.

'You idiot!' shouted Jordan. His voice was sharp. 'First the paint on the van, and now this—Shea had the right idea all along.'

'Calm down,' said Kitty. 'The lad hasn't said anything.'

'But he was about to,' said Jordan. He walked back

towards the fire, kicking a clump of sand. It sprayed up and floated back towards me, landing on my tongue.

'I didn't say anything,' said Benji. He looked scared.

'I know,' said Kitty. 'But I think you should take Star home.'

'I don't want to go,' I said. I couldn't understand what had happened. I couldn't understand how everything had changed.

'No, she's right,' said Benji. 'Let's go. It's time.'

The sky was quickly getting lighter. Not the usual light. Not yellow and pale blue, but crimson and orange.

'Red sky in the morning,' said Kitty, moving her hand across her face, pushing away a curl of smoke from her cigarette. 'Take care, Star,' she said. 'Take great care.'

'I don't want to go,' I said again.

Benji grabbed my arm. 'Come on,' he said.

We walked through the dunes. The sun began to rise over the sea. It was red, like Kitty said: a blood orange, casting pink light onto the sand. It was the first proper sunrise I had seen. And for me, it didn't signify the breaking of a new day, but the end of something.

'What happened?' I asked.

'They don't think we should be friends anymore,' he said.

'Why not?'

'Because we're too different, from different places.' He was agitated; something buzzed around his head. 'They've got it wrong.'

'Got what wrong?'

'I'm …' he began. Then he stopped. 'It doesn't matter.'

'It does matter,' I said. 'Tell me. What have you done wrong? What's so bad about us being friends?'

'Because I'm not from the same place as you—we're supposed to stay separate. They think I've shown you things, but I haven't, have I? Oh, I can't remember. Everything goes blurry when I'm with you.'

He wasn't making sense; talking to someone who wasn't there, frantically searching for an answer.

'Have I done something wrong?' I said.

'It's not about you, Star,' he said.

'Then what's it about?'

'It's about …' he started. Again, he stopped himself. 'It's about what it's always been about—it's about magic.'

'What?' he wasn't making much sense.

'That's all, Star. That's all it's ever been about.'

He suddenly pulled me in for a hug and squeezed me really tightly. I could smell the side of his neck, behind his ear. He smelt like a boy should smell—like outside.

‘Don’t worry about what they said,’ he said. ‘We’re like a family—we argue all of the time. We’ll sort it out.’

‘Are you sure?’ I asked. He nodded, and I suddenly understood his need for words, always. Silence wasn’t enough; a nod and a weak smile was nothing compared to real confirmation. ‘Say yes,’ I said.

‘Yes.’

‘I’ll see you after breakfast?’ I said. ‘You’ll be waiting, on the beach?’

‘Yes,’ he said. ‘I’ll be there.’

I pushed open the garden gate and crept down the side of the cottage. Then I climbed through the window and landed face-first on the bed.

The argument he had with his friends definitely had something to do with Shea disappearing. There was something going on that they were trying to hide from me—there was no doubt in my mind about that.

I wondered if they would be joining her tonight. I wondered if I had seen them all for the last time.

My head left the pillow as I sprang forward, unable to lie still at the thought. That would be horrible.

My tired eyes darted around the room, looking for something, anything, to focus on, to stop the onset of panic. I saw my baseball shirt, scrunched up in the corner, the same one I had worn the first night I went to the beach. I remembered how that felt—how exciting and dangerous.

Now, sneaking about under Dad's nose was just necessary; a part of my life, the only way I could do what I needed to do. But that would be over soon. Everything would be over soon.

I was so preoccupied with thinking that I didn't notice the floorboards in the hallway creak. I didn't notice the breeze blow under the gap in the door, and I didn't notice a hand pressing against the wood.

It slowly opened, and his face appeared, sunken and angry. The red sun turned him into fury.

'We need to talk,' he said.

He moved into the room and pressed the door closed behind him.

Twelve.

He stood in the doorway, coloured by fire. My heart began to punch me in the back. Hearts weren't supposed to do that. I felt dizzy. My hands were clammy. I couldn't take in enough breath.

Just like that, I was the old me again. The scared me. The person I thought I had left in Newcastle.

'Where have you been?' he asked. I couldn't answer. My throat filled with barbed wire, twisted and sharp—a warning to any words that passed through it. 'Star,' he said, taking a step forward. I instinctively moved back. 'Where have you been?'

His lined face flooded with blood in the rising sunlight, more than angry, more than fierce. Each deep crease filled with shadows. He looked terrifying, but also terrified. 'Where have you been?' he asked again. He punched out each word through gritted teeth.

I realised then that he already knew where I had been. He had been watching me. Spying. I could see it in his eyes. Finally see him.

He came closer and stood at the end of the bed, where Mam always stood. I didn't want him there. I didn't want him in my room. He wasn't Mam. He would never be her. Never be enough.

A word formed somewhere around my heart, made from blood and heat and anger. It rose up like the red sun, towards my throat, and burned through. 'Out,' I said.

'With who?' he asked, too quickly.

I didn't answer. I wouldn't give him what he wanted. What he already knew.

'You know, it's funny,' he said, 'because I bumped into a family in the village this afternoon. Two girls—about your age, blonde hair, just like you described, on their way to the Kayaking Club down on the beach. I asked if they knew where you were—if they recognised you from the club at all. Do you know what they said?'

I was backed into a corner. I had to fight. 'You've been spying,' I said.

'I've been trying to look after you,' he said.

Is that what he called it? My life was crumbling to pieces;

my only friends in the world were leaving and I couldn't spend time with them because I had to keep him happy. I had to pander to him. I had to do whatever he told me to. Everything was his fault.

'No, you haven't,' I said. 'You never have.'

He blinked twice. The change in him snapped into the room, like a door slamming. He was no longer angry. No longer red. Just confused. The blood rushed from his face. 'What?' he said.

'You never look after me,' I said. 'I look after myself.'

'Is that right?' he began, almost laughing; almost teasing. *Why couldn't he take me seriously?* I wasn't a kid anymore. I was fourteen and a half. 'Do you know what, Star?' he continued, 'I am sick of this. I brought you here because I could see you were struggling at home. I thought it was the best thing for you. And we've done everything you wanted—you didn't want to go to the beach, so we didn't go to the beach; you wanted some independence, so we left you alone. All I've asked is that you stay away from those people in the caravan, because they're not good people. And what do you do?'

'You don't know anything,' I said. I was shouting. So much noise felt alien in my throat. It hurt. My words were like knives, cutting through the barbed wire that was already there.

I was ferocious, a caged animal. Ruled by fear. All I could do was lash out. I had never had a confrontation in my life. I had never had the courage to bite back. Never had something worth biting back for.

'No, Star,' he said. '*You* don't know anything. You don't think about anyone else but yourself, and I've had enough of it.'

He moved away from the end of the bed, and I pressed further into the headboard behind me.

I waited. Waited for him to shout, waited for him to shut me up like he always did.

But the weirdest thing happened; the fight seemed to leave him too quickly. He walked towards the door, running his hands down his face. 'I'm not talking about this now,' he said. He didn't even look at me. 'I need to go to bed.'

I felt weightless. Stopped in my tracks. Deprived of finally voicing my feelings to the one person who could change things. He couldn't just walk into my room and shout his commands then leave. I had to be able to defend myself. I had to be able to speak.

'He's my best friend,' I said. My voice was frailer. 'I'll run away with him.' I was scrambling for power. Scrambling to be his equal. Scrambling to have a say in my own life. 'I won't stop seeing him.'

'You will,' he said.

'You don't get it—I need him, I need them. They're the only ones who get me. They're the only ones who know what it's like to be like me. You haven't got a clue.'

His chin was low to his chest. His shoulders rising up and down. 'What are you talking about?' he said. 'What lies have they been telling you?'

'It's not lies—it's magic!' I knew how stupid I sounded.

He laughed. 'Of course it is, Star. Life's just all magic and rainbows.'

'Don't laugh,' I said.

'Oh, get a grip, man, will you? They're wanderers—they're bloody professional liars. Do you seriously think they're your friends, Star? I bet they saw you coming, nice lad like you.'

'Stop it.' I felt my resolve slip. He knew exactly what to say. He knew my weaknesses. It was too easy for me to think it had never been real. It was too easy for me to think that they weren't really my friends. After all, who would want to be friends with a boy like me?

'What are you going to do? Are you going to live in a caravan for the rest of your life? Are you going to run away and join the circus—is that why you've got all that glitter on your face? Have you turned into a fairy now, eh?'

'Why do you have to say that?' I shouted. 'Why can't anybody ever think of anything else to say? Fine, yes. I'm a fairy just like them. The biggest fairy in Newcastle, the lads on the estate call me.'

'What?'

'That's what they call me—a fairy. Does that bother you? Are you ashamed that your son's a fairy?'

'This ends now,' he said.

'No, it doesn't—it doesn't just end, Dad, it won't just pass. This is who I am. Do you hear me? I'm like them—I'm not like the other lads. I don't want to be like the other lads. I don't want to be like you.'

'You're my son and I say this ends now!'

'I wish I wasn't your son,' I shouted. 'I wish you hadn't come here. I wish it was you that was dead and not Mam!'

Silence.

He did nothing. Just stared.

We weren't trying to protect each other any more. We weren't trying to hide the truth so the other didn't get upset. We were fighting until one of us was too damaged to fight back. And it looked like I had won. And it felt horrible to win against him like that.

He turned to face the door, 'We're going back to Newcastle tomorrow,' he said, steadily. 'As soon as I can arrange the tickets.'

'What? No. You can't make me—'

'That's enough!' he shouted. His eyes were wet. 'I don't want to hear another bloody word out of you.'

He disappeared behind the door, slamming it shut.

An echo rang off the walls.

Everything was over. Just like that. My new life, Benji, the friendship, the things I had wanted for such a long time. It all just went away.

The clock in the village stopped chiming in the hours. The breeze outside stopped blowing and the sun got stuck behind the dunes. It was like a grey cloth had been lowered over my eyes. All the new colours I had discovered muted. All the light turned to dark. And I was the source. Darkness spilled out of my fingertips, out of my eyelashes. It swirled around me like a cloud until it suffocated everything else.

I was space. I was air. I was nothing.

Nothing.

Nothing.

Baby. Her voice was different. Mocking. *What's wrong?* I couldn't see her. She was just a whisper in the black, a rustling of the wind in the bushes, or a sway of the curtains. *You're stronger than this, baby. You're stronger than me.*

'I'm not,' I said. 'I'm not anything.'

My pillow was wet. The back of my stomach ached with hunger and sadness.

Will you do something for me? she asked.

It wasn't her real voice. It was the one that only existed in my head; a trick of the light or a creak in the dark—broken and cracked. I wouldn't do anything for a voice I didn't know.

Focus on people's innocence, not their guilt, she said. *Will you do that?*

'What do you mean?' I asked.

There was no reply. That wasn't her style. I didn't get to use her as I wished; I didn't get to rely on her. She came and went as she pleased, just like she did when she was alive. She left as quickly as she came, and all I could do was wait for her.

I flicked the curtains open and I saw the moon, fat and round and glowing white. A group of thin clouds spread around it, not enough to throw shade as they slid slowly past.

My tongue tasted bitter and dry, and I could feel every rib as my lungs moved slowly up and down, gradually gaining momentum.

The church bell in the village chimed three times. I must have slept all day. And now it was the morning before I had to leave Beadnell forever.

I sat forward. Clouds bled over my eyes as the blood rushed to my head. I blinked until my bedroom returned. I ran my fingers through my knotty hair and tied it high on top of my head with a bobble I kept around my wrist.

My first proper thought was of him, even though I was supposed to forget him now.

My next thought was heavier. I remembered the argument with Dad. We had both said things we shouldn't. I felt bad about that—not that it really mattered; we were about to go back to a lifetime of ignoring each other anyway.

I couldn't go back to that. There had to be something else.

My next decision came to me in the flicker of a star, in a feeling that, surprisingly, still burned in the pit of my stomach.

I had to tell Benji what had happened. He would know what to do. He always had the answers. He made even the heaviest of my thoughts light.

I threw off the bed sheets and pressed my palms against my temples, willing the sudden pain to go away. I rubbed the crusty tears from my eyes and snatched in a breath through my nostrils. Then I grabbed the chair by my bed and wedged it against the door.

With shaking hands, I opened the window quietly, keeping the curtains drawn, and jumped into the night; jumped into the unknown, hoping he would be there to catch my fall.

The faces sitting around the fire weren't the ones I knew. They were regular, not unusual at all, with widespread grins and sun-freckled noses. The orange light from the flames complemented their healthy skin and golden, sun-bleached hair. They all looked the same, like clones: an army of perfect teeth and high cheekbones.

I could tell by the state of the fire, by the way the smoke moved—straight up in solid clouds—that it didn't belong to them, to the wanderers. Their fire didn't do that; it danced and swirled and laughed sometimes as the peppery smoke curled and changed colour.

There was nothing familiar about this one. It belonged to a group of boys, probably from the holiday homes by the other beach—the neat wooden boxes with neat square lawns outside and the same car parked in each driveway. There was nothing special about boys like them—not to me, anyway. Not anymore.

I hid in the dunes, looking down onto the sand and the black water. The beach wasn't the same place without him. It wasn't our place anymore. I could feel the change in the colder air and in the voices that ran along the water's edge.

I realised then that it was never ours to begin with. We had been allocated a whisper of time, a flash of a moment, and it was over now. I suddenly felt scared. If he wasn't at the beach, if he wasn't the boy waiting for me on the sand, by the dunes, then I didn't know who he was.

I wasn't sure what came next.

I looked to the far side, where the sea curled round and met the harbour wall. The moon shone down on the limekilns, outlining their unusual shape. The first day we had properly met was by the harbour. The day he saved me from drowning, or from worse—a summer spent with a group of boys who would never accept me; the summer I'd thought I wanted. It was a sentimental place. I wondered if he would be there—if he cared that much.

If I knew him at all, if the summer had meant even a fraction of what I thought it did, then he had to be somewhere here. He wouldn't just go without saying goodbye.

I ran down the dunes, swishing the long grass out of my way. I didn't care if anybody saw me—I didn't care if Dad found out. I had to get to him and tell him what had happened.

Up on the harbour wall, the night air stank of seaweed and stagnant water. I looked over the edge and saw the sea, climbing and falling, teasing the ropes that hung from giant metal rings by pulling them forward and pushing them back as if there were some other force at play below the surface. I looked further, walking right to the edge, my shoelaces hanging over the side. There was something enticing about the black water, about the completeness of it. I could almost hear it calling my name, beckoning me in to it. Something flashed at the bottom; a face, maybe, with yellow eyes and pockmarked skin, or a selkie waiting to drag me into nothing.

I peered over further, bending towards it. I couldn't stop myself. Didn't want to. Maybe it made sense that I could go there and none of this would matter any more. Maybe this was always what I was supposed to do.

I took a deep breath and closed my eyes.

Someone grabbed my wrist and pulled me back. 'What are you doing?' he said.

I turned to see him, his face frozen by the moonlight. 'I had to see you,' I said. I was shaking.

'Were you going to jump?' He looked over the side.

'No,' I said. And I was shocked that I nearly had. I began to really shake.

'The sea isn't as kind at night.' He ran his hands through his hair and shook it so it fell, thick and stringy, on his face. It was wet. He pulled me along the harbour wall towards the limekilns and we hid inside.

I had missed him, even though it couldn't have even been a day. I couldn't get through forever without him. The thought of how empty I would be without him stabbed into me.

'Something's wrong,' he said.

I had to tell him what had happened—what Dad had said. I had so much to say, but I couldn't voice a single word. It was like I had forgotten. My throat became thin and soft, like the stem of a flower. If words passed through, they would definitely break it. I was scared, but I had to say something. This could have been our very last night together. I needed him to help me. 'Benji—'

'Come with me,' he said.

'What?'

'Come with me,' he said again. 'We can go. Tonight. By the time the morning comes, we can be long gone, and this won't matter anymore.' He held out his hand. It was shaking, like mine. 'Come with me and everything will change for you, just like you want it to.'

I didn't move. I wanted to go to him—I had never wanted something more—but I couldn't allow myself to. Not straight away. I had been brave this summer, braver than I ever thought I could be, but was I brave enough to do this?

He took my hand. 'Wait,' I said, placing mine on top of

his. 'Where will we go?'

'It doesn't matter,' he said. 'We can go anywhere. We can go to other beaches and mountains and waterfalls that no one knows about. It doesn't matter—we'll be together. Me and you.'

Stories, and adventures, and pictures of a perfect future where there were no cares just weren't enough. Lies weren't enough. It was time for truth. I needed that from him. This was serious—we needed more than his magic.

He pulled me along the harbour wall. The wind had grown; it threw my hair into my face. The sea was wilder than I had seen it. It thundered into the jagged black rocks and leapt into the air before spraying on the concrete like heavy raindrops. Above, clouds began to move over the moon, blocking out its light. A storm was coming, but this one wasn't to clear the air or smooth the stones; this one wasn't to break the heat or clean the ground. This one was to tear it up.

He led me onto the beach and we ran towards the dunes. My trainers sank into the soft sand, making it harder to run, harder to move forward, as if I were running in a dream.

It felt wrong. I was scared of so many things. I needed to know how this would turn out. 'Wait,' I said, 'where are we going?'

He looked over his shoulder without stopping; still pulling

me further towards a future I didn't know I wanted. He was running away from something. His time had run out. He was frantic. Scrambling. I could see he had no plan. I wanted him to say he knew exactly where we would go.

But that wasn't him—he acted on impulse. He was wild. He was the sky and the sea, the wind and the river; he couldn't stay in one place. He feared that as much as I feared the uncertainty of what came next.

'I can't,' I said.

'What?'

'I can't come with you tonight.'

'What are you talking about? Of course you can.'

I wasn't like him. I wasn't confident or carefree. I cared about a lot of things.

I realised then that, though I hated it at times, and though the last two years there had been miserable, I had roots that ran deep under the shoebox-sized house on the estate. It was my home, whether I liked it or not. It was the last place I saw her; it was where we laughed together for the last time; it was where I held her and smelt her hair for the last time. I couldn't just turn my back on that. 'I can't come with you,' I said again. Saying it out loud helped.

'You can,' he said. 'Of course you can.'

'I can't. Not now—I need some time to think.'

'But there isn't any time.'

'I know.'

'You're free, Star. The only thing stopping you is you. I thought you'd worked that out. I'm offering you the chance to live your life—really live your life. Why wouldn't you want to do that?'

I looked into his green eyes, the eyes that had stopped me in my tracks the first day I saw him on the field between the beach and the cottage; the field we were standing on now. I could sort of see a future for us in them. I could see sunshine and adventures. But I couldn't see the one thing I needed. I couldn't see certainty. I couldn't see home. And something told me that I never would—that he would give me all of the excitement I ever needed, but I would never have the ground under my feet.

I pulled my hand out of his. 'I can't,' I said.

'You can,' he said. He was angry. I didn't understand.

'What's wrong?' I asked. There was more to this than us leaving together. I could feel it. He was running from something. He was scared. 'Have you done something?'

'Have I done something?' he said. We weren't moving anymore; weren't doing anything. We were just standing, trapped in limbo, caught between the future and the past. 'Are you joking? Like—seriously, haven't you worked it out yet?'

'Worked what out?' I asked.

'The paint on the caravan,' he said. 'I did it. I wrote those words.'

'What do you mean?' I said.

'I wanted you to see it. I wanted you to know.'

'Wanted me to know what?'

He scratched his fingertips down his cheeks. 'Are you really that stupid, Star?' he said.

His words stabbed my chest. 'Don't call me that.'

'I've risked everything for you, absolutely everything. More than you've even bothered to work out. Shea has left—everyone is falling apart. I've risked everything, and you're just walking away like it all never happened.'

'I'm not! We can still see each other on weekends and—'

'No, we can't! We can't do any of that stuff. It's now or nothing.'

'I can't,' I said.

'Why not?'

'Because I'm scared she won't be able to find me.' The words came out of me without thinking about them. How could I see Mam when I was so far away from familiarity? Before long, she would become a faint memory that belonged to someone else. I didn't want that. I still needed her.

'Fine,' he said, 'sit in your bedroom and pretend for the

rest of your life. I'm done with you.'

'You don't mean that,' I said, in a voice that was all too familiar.

'Do you know what, Star?' he continued, ignoring me. 'No matter how much you wish it, no matter how much you stay in there on your own, pretending, no matter how much you think you can hear her voice, it's never going to bring her back. It's never real. She's gone.'

She's gone. Two words I feared above anything else. The words I never wanted to hear. Trigger words. *She's gone.* I remembered being told, at school, sitting in the cold headteacher's office for ages because none of them were brave enough to say it. *She's gone.* The day my world came crashing down around me. *She's gone.* The words that stole my voice, and now he was using them on me. Using them to hurt me.

Suddenly, I was the one making things up. I was the one living in a dream world. I had asked him for truth and he had given it to me.

I turned away. He grabbed the top part of my arm, turning me around to face him. 'Where are you going?' he said.

I pushed him off with strength I didn't know I had and continued to walk. My skin burned and the hairs on the back of my neck stood on end. I didn't need to feel like this again. I didn't need this much pain in my life.

'Hey,' he said.

'I've told you things I've never told anyone before,' I said, 'and now you're throwing them back at me like that?' I stared right at him, right through him, to his heart beating underneath his t-shirt. He knew he had crossed a line; he knew he had pushed me too far.

'Ah, I didn't mean—'

'No one ever does, do they? No one ever means to say the nasty things. They just slip out. Do you know what? You're just like every other boy. There's nothing special about you.'

I turned my back on him, too angry to look at his face, and began to walk away. 'That's just perfect,' he shouted after me. 'Fine—go and sit in your room with your dead mam. See if I care.'

I kicked the back gate open and allowed it to slam shut. I opened the back door and ran through the kitchen, knocking over a glass vase as I passed. It smashed into pieces, throwing shards across the floor. Someone called my name. I didn't know who; the storm inside my head was even louder than the one outside, and it was finally ready to break.

Thirteen.

I thudded across the floorboards, smashing the bedroom door against the wall, sending the chair flying. I felt so hot; so angry. I couldn't keep still. I couldn't be silent any more. I was full of fire. I was the storm. I was rage and smashing waves and jagged rocks. I was thunder and white light and thick black clouds. I had to hurt things as much as I was hurting. I had to let the noise on the inside come out. I wanted to shake the house to the ground.

Outside, a flash of white exploded at my window. I stood watching. Waiting. I wanted more of it, more energy from the sky and the clouds and the ground.

My mouth felt strange, as if my teeth were just stones. I wanted to grit them, clench them, crunch them to sand. My whole body felt harder, like I could smash the room to pieces with my fists or my forehead.

And the person I'd thought I was had got completely lost amongst it all.

The storm came on quick and fast. Thunder galloped across the sea like racehorses, over the field and in through my bedroom window. Shaking the walls. Thick clouds squeezed the light from the night, turning it to darkness. A flicker of lightning—twisted and fast—shot into them, tearing across the sky like an intricate network of veins around a heart.

I wanted to see everything. I wanted to see what the world looked like when it was angry, because I was angry.

The rain came, heavy, tearing up the fleshy ground and beating the stones. It sprayed in through my open window, covering my face. It was dirty rain. Earth rain. The clouds came nearer, hanging heavily over the ground. The lightning and thunder made me more dangerous. I had nothing to lose. I had already lost so much. I couldn't hold on to any of it anymore—Mam, Dad, Benji; I surrendered everything I felt about them to the storm. I wanted to tear at it with my teeth.

Thunder shouted and I shouted with it. Noise vibrated in my chest and spewed out of my mouth. I yelled my name, over and over again. I yelled his name. I called him every horrible thing I could think of, and I wanted him to hear me. I wanted the little caravan to wash away on a river of my words.

I had trusted him. I had told him things I had never spoken about, and he had used my deepest secrets against me; used them to hurt me. He was like all the other boys, probably worse, because he had hurt me in a much deeper way—a cleverer way.

I screamed for Mam. I asked the clouds, the lightning, the thunder why she had to go. Tears ran down my cheeks, running salt rivers over my cracked lips. I screamed and cried and laughed and allowed my voice to vibrate in my chest, filling my heart with electricity. I wasn't used to that. I had held so much back—stifled so many feelings, and they were all coming out, a lifetime's worth of pain, throbbing until my face and hands did the same.

And the storm raged on, and so did I. I had to be heard. I asked the sky again why she had to go. *Why wasn't there an answer? Why didn't anybody ever have an answer?*

I blamed the clouds and the rain and the lightning, and they fought back; they didn't try to calm me, or tell me to bury my anger further down, so deep that I couldn't find it again. I had found the perfect sparring partner in the storm.

I wanted to be louder than the thunder. I wanted to be heard above the noise. I wanted to be important enough.

I felt a surge of cold air press against my back, and someone grabbed me from behind. Some other storm, some other power, came from the other side of my bedroom; came to fight the one inside of me that wanted to shatter me to pieces. I struggled against it; struggled against them, throwing my arms about so they couldn't get too close. I didn't need anyone. I knew how to look after myself.

They held me as I struggled and didn't let go. They held fast. Got tighter. Held me with more than what they were; with more than arms and fingers. They surrounded me in something I hadn't felt for a long time. Something powerful. I tried to fight against it, tried to pretend I didn't need it.

But my rage couldn't survive in its presence. It broke into chunks, like clouds, awkwardly moving away from the moon, awkwardly moving around me, causing my shoulders to shunt up and down, causing my mouth to quiver around my cries.

I came back. I was me again—detached from the storm, and fragile. The smell of aftershave and Fox's mints swirled around me and I became softer. I became blood and bones and moving parts. I became human.

I leant forward and fell into that smell; fell into him. My dad.

I dived into us, into our world before, filled with memories of laughter. I swam in them, seeing each one afresh with more than my eyes. Seeing them with the things Benji had shown me. One by one they came to life again; even the ones I had buried really deeply.

I was a kid again. I was the person who knew they were loved; the person who didn't have to think about things like bravery, and risks—they weren't necessary, didn't exist yet. There was only this. My world.

'You've always been special,' he said, holding me tightly. I couldn't move. Couldn't stop crying for all the things I had never cried about. 'Right from the first moment you came into this world.' He kissed my forehead and wiped away my tears with his fingertips. He was crying too, but his face didn't look sad. It didn't look lined and gaunt like it usually did—his cheeks were flushed and his eyes sparkling as he went somewhere to find his memories too.

'The last two years have been horrible, son. I've been so desperate for her mistakes not to become yours that I've forgotten what's important. I'm sorry. Those things I said earlier—I didn't mean them at all. I love you, Star. My boy.'

I had wanted to hear that for so long. I didn't know how much until I felt his words, sticking into my joints and moving through my bones. Making me real again. He was the one I had needed all along. He knew how to fix me. And he had always been there.

'I'm …' I began, my voice small again, 'I'm sorry.'

'You're fourteen, Star,' he said. 'Fourteen. You have

nothing to be sorry for.'

'I've been horrible to you,' I said.

'And I was horrible to my parents when I was fourteen. I'm sure your Mam was too.' He dropped his eyes, and I saw it. His pain.

I could finally see him for what he was: a parent trying his best to raise a kid on his own. The colour of his skin; the lost expression across his forehead, they were new things—things that came after Mam had gone. Why hadn't I noticed—why didn't I know he was hurting too? We were two broken people, two halves of the same thing, the same family. We needed each other.

Focus on his innocence, said a voice. *He needs you, and you him.*

Mam stood right behind him, her face flushed and pretty. She looked better than I had seen her. A gentle sort of light—not the sun, but the moon; the pressing of silver against pale blue hovered around her head, highlighting her heart-shaped face.

I stared at her from Dad's arms as the tears grew sticky on my cheeks. 'What would you say to her?' I asked. 'If she was here, what would you say?'

His chest vibrated once against my ear as a thin laugh stuck in his throat. 'Hindsight is a wonderful thing,' he said.

'I've gone over that day in my head too many times. I had no idea things had got so bad. I suppose I'll have to live with that for the rest of my life.'

Mam was still smiling at me. Her pale face was unmoving but her long hair was swaying around it. She looked like she was underwater, but she wasn't struggling anymore. She was at peace. 'But what would you say?' I asked again. I knew she wouldn't stay forever. I knew she came and went as she pleased. I wanted her to hear what Dad had to say.

'I suppose I'd say …' he began, 'I suppose I'd just say *I love you.*'

I looked up to Mam, to see if she had heard it, to see if the words had changed her.

She had moved away. She stood in the doorway now, framed by wood and straight lines. No longer close enough to hear us. She was going somewhere. *Never change*, she said. She smiled again. Her lips spread across her pretty face.

It wasn't enough; I needed to know she had heard what Dad had said. I was just about to ask him to say it again when she said: *look after him. He's precious to me.* She brought her hand up to her mouth and pressed her fingers against her pursed lips, then blew a kiss. I felt it land between my eyebrows, warming my skin. *I love you, my baby. My Star.*

I closed my eyes tightly, trying to make the moment last

for as long as I could. Trying to keep it with me always.

I knew she was going forever. She had to—things had to change. I realised I wasn't sad about that. I wanted it. Dad and me couldn't go on the way we were; we had to find a way to move on.

It was funny how close I was to this; how breaking point was this near.

I didn't feel panicky or scared, because she wasn't real—not the real that I needed, anyway. Benji was right, even though his words cut me into pieces. Even though his words meant that he had lost my trust. I couldn't waste any more of my life clinging on to the ghosts of my past when I had real people in my present who cared about me; who needed me. Mam would always be with me, because I would make sure of it. I didn't need a ghost to tell me that I was loved.

'She loves you too,' I said, squeezing him tighter. It felt good doing that.

He snatched in a breath to say something; his stomach expanded, but no words came. There wasn't anything to say. All he had to do was listen and accept it.

We sat for ages, just holding each other as he stroked my hair with his hand.

Outside, the clouds unclasped the full moon, moving away to other places and other people that needed them. The storm was really over this time, and it had been a long time coming. I had raged like the North Sea. Smashed and clapped and yelled my hurt out of me, and Dad had done the same. Two years of silence had resulted in deafening noise; deafening anger, and now it was time to let go and leave the past behind, where it belonged.

Fourteen.

The sun woke me early that morning.

The world outside of my window was different. The grass that had dried and snapped, the puddles that had drained and cracked came back to life in a surge of colour and mud as waspish clouds hurried over pale blue. The air was cleaner. Wetter. Less thick. The storm had given the earth exactly what it needed. Gone was the warm wind, soft and creamy. Gone was the stillness of summer. Things were moving again.

A sharp, oncoming chill backed the air. It blew onto my morning face and tingled it awake. There was no time for sentimentality. No time to stare at the memories made while the sun shone; no time to look back and imagine. Life didn't work like that.

The caravan had gone.

It had left nothing behind, as if it hadn't been there at all. No grooves in the mud, no blackened grass where the fire burned on the ground outside of it, and no lines across the green where the Range Rover had pulled it away. Pulled it to the next place, wherever that was. The field behind the cottage had never felt so huge.

I didn't know what to think. Didn't know how to feel. The thing I had been worried about, not even twenty-four hours earlier, had happened. I should have been terrified. I should have felt alone again.

But I didn't.

The change was happening in more places than outside my window. I felt it in the blood that ran through me more lightly than it had for two years. I was back in a place where I felt safe. The heaviness I had been carrying around with me had been lifted away by the one person I never thought would do that.

Dad sat at the table in the garden, neat and calm. Smiling. His pale shirt, as crisp and as clean as the morning, was buttoned up to the neck. His face looked nowhere near as harsh—he looked like he had slept really well. I didn't have to look further into his eyes to search for him. I didn't have to squint and pretend. He was there all right, plain as day.

'Morning,' he said.

‘Morning,’ I said.

I felt awkward. A lot had been said last night, and I knew mornings were different. In the light of day, people changed.

I sensed he recognised it in me. He could see me just as clearly as I could him, I realised. He knew me just as well. Probably better. I had never thought about it before, but I wondered if all the times I had spent staring into his dark eyes, looking for the person I knew behind them, he was doing the same to me; searching for me in the dark.

I had spent so long blaming him. I was embarrassed about that. He had been there the whole time, as sturdy as a rock, and I hadn’t treated him well at all.

I took a seat opposite him at the table. ‘I feel good this morning,’ I said. ‘How do you feel?’

‘Alright,’ he said.

‘Good,’ I said. ‘It was a bad storm last night, wasn’t it?’

‘Star,’ he said, ‘I don’t want you to feel bad about any of this. It’s over now.’

‘Okay.’

‘Let’s draw a line under it. I don’t want to think about the past anymore—I’m sick of it. You’ve got your whole life ahead of you.’

‘Okay.’

He glugged his cup of coffee and I reached for a sandwich,

tearing a corner off the bread and twisting it around it my fingers.

'They were my friends,' I said. I knew we were supposed to be placating each other. I knew we were supposed to be starting afresh. But I just wanted to be clear. We could move on, and I wanted that, but I needed him to acknowledge the part they played in all of this. 'I know you didn't like them—'

'I'm sorry about that,' he said. 'I thought I was doing the right thing—being a good parent. You're just so like her, Star … I thought if you got mixed up with people like that you'd run off or do something stupid or something.'

'I thought about it,' I said.

'But you didn't.'

'No.'

'Why?'

'I don't know. Maybe I'm not as much like her as you think.'

He nodded, smiling. It turned out his fears were my fears. I worried I was exactly the same as her too. I worried that I would do what she had done, because I understood her darkness sometimes. But I wasn't just her. I'd had two parents. One of them had been wild and funny and impulsive, but the other was steadfast and caring and sensitive. Only I hadn't known that until now.

'Look,' I began, 'I have to be able to make my own mistakes. I'm not a kid anymore.'

'Okay,' he said. 'I get it. Just talk to me, really, about anything. If you're sad, if you're having a hard time with the lads at school—anything. I want you to know that you can tell me. I've not exactly been the best dad in the world. I want you to know that I support you—I suppose that's what I'm saying.'

I knew that. There were parts of him I understood, just like there were parts of Mam I understood. I could feel every word he said, as if I had said them; like they weren't made out of breath and warmth but were real things that I could hold in my hands.

The time had come to tell him.

'Dad,' I began. 'I think I'm different.'

He nodded.

'No, what I mean is—I'm not like other boys. I don't feel like a boy. I don't like sports. I don't fancy girls.'

'Okay.'

'I don't know what that means. Some days I'm so confused I don't know what anything means. Then some days I can see myself really clearly. More so since I met them.'

I wasn't going to talk about Benji and his friends too much. This wasn't about them anymore; it was far bigger than that. But it was time to be honest. No pretence; no lies; no magic, even—just truth. Clean, clear, truth.

'The people in the caravan, you mean?' he said.

'Yes.'

'I understand.'

'You do?'

'Look, I'm not so old that I don't remember what it's like to meet someone on Beadnell beach.'

'What do you mean?' I asked.

'I grew up in this house, Star,' he said. 'I spent my teenage years climbing out of my window to go and meet some girl.'

'Alright, too much information,' I said, waving my hands, 'really.'

He smiled, and I saw a flash in his eyes for the first time in ages. It made me smile too. 'I'm only sorry that I forgot,' he said.

'Me too,' I said.

'Hey,' he said. He flicked a piece of bread at me. 'I know you're different, Star. You always have been, and, well, I'm here for you.'

I knew I had work to do—I knew the journey to finding out who I really was wouldn't necessarily be as easy as it was for most other people. I wasn't even sure where I was going to end up. But knowing that I had a parent in my life who cared for and supported me—who wanted the best for me—gave me the safety net I needed to really explore myself without worrying about messing it all up. It felt amazing, in a way that only something really unexpected can.

'Thanks, Dad,' I said.

Shuna walked through the French doors, as bright and as colourful as she was the first day I met her, bringing with her the smell of incense on the hem of her kaftan. 'Ah,' she said, smiling from one side of her haircut to the other. 'I'm glad to see you finally got what you asked for, Toby.'

'Maybe,' Dad said.

'What are you talking about?' I asked.

'Your dad got his wish,' said Shuna.

'What?' I said.

'Shuna has this daft theory,' said Dad, awkwardly shuffling in his seat.

'It's only daft if you choose to look at it that way,' said Shuna.

'The night before we came here,' Dad said in a low voice, clearly wanting to tell it in his own words before Shuna embellished, 'the last night at home, in Newcastle, I heard you crying in your room.' I remembered that night. It was right at the beginning of summer, when I was hopeless, when the only future I could see involved staring at the four walls of my bedroom until the new school year started. 'I sat on the side of my bed and, well, I suppose I made a wish. I don't know why, I don't know where it came from. I didn't think anything of it then, but Shuna has reminded me of it ever since I told her—which I'm massively regretting now, Star, I can tell you.'

'That's not the full story,' said Shuna. 'You're forgetting to mention that on that same night, I met a girl in the village—someone I've never seen before, or seen since, I might add—who told me that I should visit my brother; that I should bring him here because he needed to remember what a summer here was like. I got the first train out of Berwick the next day.'

'It's a long way to travel on the advice of a stranger,' said Dad.

'Yes, but thank goodness I did.'

I couldn't imagine Dad making a wish. I couldn't imagine him even considering that as an option. 'What did you wish for?' I asked.

'I can't remember what I said exactly,' he said. 'I just remembered wanting you to talk to me about whatever was upsetting you—and wanting to be as close to you as we were before, you know, before your mam went.'

I had been so blind to him. I had no idea back then that he cared so much. No idea that he was sitting on the other side of the wall, wishing for my happiness; wanting to talk to me about the things that made me sad. *Why didn't he speak to me then?*

But then, I wondered if I would have been able to hear him. I wondered if the summer had needed to happen the way it did, so we could properly see each other again.

'The fae folk heard your wish,' said Shuna.

'Well the girl in the village certainly did,' said Dad, a smirk spread across his face. 'She didn't come from the Scotswood Estate, did she?'

'What did she look like?' I asked. Something clicked on in my head; something that, initially, I thought I knew nothing about, but at the same time, I had known about all along.

'Oh, I can't really remember,' said Shuna.

And right away I knew. It always happened when I saw them too—I couldn't describe them to anyone else. Like I wasn't allowed to. 'She had red hair,' she said, scrambling to remember. 'Yes—it was short. And she was smoking a cigarette.'

'That could be anyone,' said Dad.

I knew that it could only be one person.

I could almost smell the cigarette smoke and almond oil in her hair, see the fire dancing in her eyes, and see her mouth forming around grey, pointed teeth.

Maybe she had spoken to Shuna by chance. Maybe the comment about visiting Dad had been a passing one. Maybe the whole thing was a coincidence. But after everything I had learned, after everything he had shown me, I didn't think so. I knew there was no such thing. The girl Shuna was talking about was Kitty.

The last cloud lifted in my mind; the final layer dissolved, and I could see everything as I was supposed to. A wish had been made, and it had been heard—heard by the voices that whispered on the wind; heard by the fire that spat out orange stars. Heard by them. And now they were gone, he was gone, because it had been granted.

It's not even his wish, that's what Shea said. They hadn't come here for me; it wasn't my voice they'd heard. It was Dad's. Solid, caring, brilliant Dad was the one who had brought magic back into our lives.

I threw my hands to my cheeks. 'The fairies heard your wish,' I said.

'What?' said Dad.

'It's true,' I said, 'the fairies heard you, Dad. They made all of this happen.'

Benji wrote the words on the caravan because he wanted me to know. *Fairy Boys*. That's why Shea got annoyed, and Jordan too; they thought he had told me their secret. Real magic existed; the world wasn't a crappy place full of liars and frauds—not everywhere, anyway. And definitely not here in

Beadnell.

'They really heard you,' I said.

'Of course they did,' he said. 'You're getting as bad as her.' He pointed at Shuna.

'Maybe I am,' I said. 'And what's wrong with that?' I brought my shoulder up to my chin and fluttered my eyelashes, just like Kitty would have done.

'You've forgotten how magical a summer in Beadnell can be,' said Shuna. 'Shame on you.'

'Alright, alright,' said Dad, 'I get it—I'm the grumpy one.'

The same old voice of reason in my head, the voice that would have kept me under my duvet in Newcastle until the end of the summer—probably until the end of time—didn't want to believe it; no matter what I had seen, no matter how changed I was. But I was done listening to that voice. I was ready to believe in magic again.

'I think we should go to the beach,' I said.

'It's a bit nippy,' said Dad.

'I don't mind if you don't. How often do we get the chance?'

'Alright,' he said. 'Ah, you'll have to get changed first, though.' He pointed to the middle of my t-shirt. I looked down and he flicked the bottom of my chin with his finger. 'Got ya!' he said.

'You're really showing your age there—nobody does that anymore.'

'Come on, that's a classic.'

'Classic is just another word for old.'

We both stood up from the table and walked through the gate.

'No, classic means it can never age,' he said.

'Not like you, then,' I said. I began to run, and he did too.

We raced across the empty field, laughing together—proper laughing, the sort of laughter that shook your ribs and buzzed in your back until you felt like you had fairy wings of your own. Dad and me, starting again in the place where he grew up and where I sort of learned to be a kid again; our world a mess of colour and possibilities and mistakes that didn't cost the earth.

We broke. Hard. Both of us did. Our past was tainted. Imperfect. That didn't mean our future had to be. *And so what if it did?* We had found a way to move through it. We had come out of the other side in a better place, an honest place. I knew that was important. I knew that what came next for me would be hard, and I knew that with him by my side, running towards our future, running towards our very own blue forever, it would be way better than anything that came before.

September

September turned summer to stone too quickly. Each day, shorter than the one before it, was bookended by a cool morning and a grey evening, as if colour had been scrubbed off the sky and only scratches of what had been there before remained. The boys stopped jumping off the pier, their laughter no longer bouncing through the limekilns; the crowds in the village thinned; Kayaking Club left the bay, taking the family with the horsey teeth with it; and the beach became a place for brisk walks instead of sunbathing and games.

I welcomed the change. I was ready for things to quieten. Ready to move on.

I missed him, though. I couldn't pretend I didn't. I felt him in my bones, in the middle of me. Not in the same way—I could survive without him. I felt stupid that I'd ever thought I couldn't. I didn't need him at my side to feel like myself; I was starting to do that all on my own. I just missed talking to him. I missed those moments we'd had together, and the silly things we'd said. I missed having a friend.

But where one person had exited my life, another came back into it.

Dad was a different person. His face and eyes and shoulders had returned to looking like those of the man I remembered. The lines on his face seemed to have smoothed out, plumped by shiny, weather-reddened skin and laughter.

He moved differently too, using his hands and arms to tell stories, and he walked with a funny bounce in his step.

We spent the last days of summer together, and in him I got back what I had been missing. A parent. He cared for me. Looked after me. Talked to me when I needed someone to listen, hugged me before I went to bed.

I knew I had Benji to thank for that—without him I wouldn't have been able to see the things I already had. I wouldn't have been able to see that Dad was hurting just as much as I was, and that we were much stronger together than we were apart.

I had spent two years in darkness, behind drawn curtains, lonely and quiet. And then my light came in an explosion; the type worlds are born from. It wasn't a candle, or a fire even; it was the sun, huge and overwhelming and needed.

But afterwards, when the light faded, I realised that life couldn't be like the sun all of the time. I had to find my own balance, and in realising that, I found out what I really needed. The sun was amazing, but flying too close to it meant I got burned.

I needed a home; I needed to feel the ground under my feet. And, above everything else, I needed to be a kid again. It was sort of sad that the things Benji had taught me ultimately meant we couldn't run away together; in finding myself, I had realised that his way of life wasn't mine. What I had now was better, though. Much better. My life wasn't perfect, and I didn't want it to be. I only wanted what I had. The things I used to worry about—being different and stuff—didn't seem important.

I had a lot to thank him for. Which sort of made me miss him more.

One morning, on my way back from collecting the morning papers, I met a familiar face in the alleyway. One I thought I would never see again.

'Hello,' he said.

I felt like I had crashed into an invisible wall. My trainers wedged into the gravel. My spine drew backwards, like an alley cat caught in the headlights of an approaching car.

'Aren't you going to say anything?' he said.

'Hello,' I said.

He didn't look the same. His once tanned skin was sallow, and his face was drawn and tired. The light no longer flashed in his eyes, copper and gold and green, but flickered quietly, as if it were about to go out.

'Do you want to come for a walk with me?' he said, shrugging his shoulders, his hands in his pockets.

His hair fell over his face, and he looked at me through it like he was hiding and didn't want to come out until I made him feel safe. I realised he was nervous.

'I have to take the papers back,' I said. I didn't have to take the papers back at all. Dad wouldn't have minded if I had turned up an hour later.

'Meet me on the beach, then,' he said, 'by the field. I'll be waiting.'

'Benji—'

'Just come.'

He had vanished before I had a chance to say any more; before I had a chance to make an excuse or tell him that my life was changing and I needed time to get used to it.

I walked into the cottage, my heart thudding like mad. I didn't want to lie to anybody. Sneaking around only made things worse.

But Dad didn't need to know I was meeting him.

'I'm back,' I announced.

'In the garden,' Dad shouted.

I walked through the kitchen, through the smell of frying bacon and sausages, into the light, into the sunshine and green grass.

I didn't have to meet him. This was my life, and it was lovely. If I didn't show up, he would get the message, and that would be the end of that—the real end, this time.

But that's the thing about the sun—once you've enjoyed a

summer, it's all you can think about. And though I knew a life of bright light and adventure wasn't a real one, it was sweeter than anything I had tasted before. And like a wasp drawn to pink jam, I couldn't resist him.

'I'm just dropping off the papers,' I said, standing by the open French doors. 'I'm going to walk down to the beach for a bit of fresh air. Won't be long.'

I wasn't lying. Walking to the beach was exactly what I was going to do. And I couldn't get there quick enough.

I knew where he would be, and because of that, I sort of knew we would meet there again—knew it wasn't completely over. That's why I had never gone to the dunes on my own since the day the caravan left, I realised. My instincts knew much better than I did.

'You came,' he said. 'I'm so glad.'

He looked different under a grey sky; far more regular. And he wasn't that much taller than me. I'd always thought he was. I realised he wasn't wearing his wings. It was like I was seeing him for the first time. Seeing the real him. I suddenly regretted coming to the beach. The memory of him was far better than the tired and fidgety boy standing in front of me.

He reached out his hand for me to follow him, and we

walked further down until tall dunes surrounded us.

I recognised the spot. It was the place I had met him and his friends properly for the first time, around the fire. I could see the faint outline of a circle drawn around blackened wood and grass, drawn in the sand by the girl with red hair.

'Where are they all?' I asked. I wondered how far wanderers travelled.

'Here and there,' he said.

'And you?'

'I'm here,' he said, smiling.

I smiled too. I hadn't expected any less from him. He never could give me a straight answer. I knew that he would never be able to open up to me like I had to him. Not really. He was exactly all of the things Dad had told me—wild and unstable. He would never have been able to be in my life—not how I wanted, anyway.

'Have you missed me?' he asked.

'I have,' I said.

'Good,' he said. 'I've missed you too.'

We sat in silence for a while. The air between us filled with awkward energy that didn't know what to do, didn't know how to move, so just hovered and waited to see which way the wind was going to blow it. I sort of felt the same. I didn't know why he had chosen to come back. I began to think it would have been better if he hadn't. 'What's this about?' I said. Apparently, I was stronger than I thought.

I felt like a new voice had formed inside of me since the last time we'd spoken; one that sat in between reason and adventure. A happy medium, maybe even a happy place, where both existed but neither ruled.

'I had to see you,' he said.

'Why?'

'So I could apologise—that thing I said. It was a bad thing to say.'

And it needed to be, I thought. His words sent me to a place where I was able to appreciate the things I had for the first time, and they had brought Dad and me together again. 'You don't have to apologise,' I said. 'You were right. Everything you said was right. Me sitting in my bedroom would never bring her back. I needed to hear it. So, thank you.'

He looked out to sea, his eyes glazed over and his head silently nodding. There were no bad feelings between us. No anger in the place where there had once been fondness. I got the feeling he had expected that.

But my life had changed so much over the summer, not just because of the brilliant time I had spent with him, doing all the things I had dreamt about, but because it had brought me home. His cruel words were the best thing that had happened to me in a long time. The other stuff was gone.

Maybe he wasn't the sun after all. Maybe he was just a candle that had briefly been made brighter by a darkness that wasn't there any more.

'You seem like your mind is made up,' he said.

'What do you want me to say?' I said.

'You don't want to be friends?'

The thought hadn't even crossed my mind. Friends. I didn't think that was possible. 'How?' I said.

'We're allowed to be friends,' he said.

'But, where?'

'Don't worry about that,' he said. 'Just say yes.'

I laughed. 'Yes.'

The first day I saw him, I knew there was something about him. We connected in a way that I couldn't explain at the time. Friends was the best way to end the summer—better than I could have hoped for, all things considered. What came after, I didn't know. I had to go back to school, and I had to continue to mend my life with Dad. That was important. If I could do that and keep him as a friend, then summer had ended in the best way possible.

I stood, and he pulled me in for a hug, like he always did. He smelt so good. Earthy. I would miss that smell. He held me a little tighter, and for a little longer than he had before, stealing a moment of time before I pulled away.

I dug my hands in my pockets, like him, and walked up the dune, stopping before I reached the top. I noticed something in my right pocket, something warm and smooth, heating the skin on my thigh. I wrapped my hand around it and pulled it upwards.

It was the holey stone, the one that chose me by the fireside. I twisted it around my fingers, holding it up to the sky. The hole in the middle expanded in the light of the sun and something came to me; something Kitty had said when she first handed it to me.

I pushed it against my eye.

I didn't know what I thought I was going to see—mermaids and giants and fairies, maybe. I would have loved that. Really. But I could only see the bay: yellow and green curving around silver and blue, swaying grass, aged limekilns, crashing waves and glass-like sand.

'Was any of it real?' I said, looking over my shoulder.

He shook his head. 'But that doesn't mean it didn't happen,' he said.

I started to laugh. He did too. His voice mixed with the wind and ran up my neck and through my hair like cool fingers, and I realised how lucky I was to have a friend like him.

I turned around to smile at him, to look into his eyes one final time and say *thank you* for everything he had done for me.

He was already gone.

When I got back to my bedroom in the cottage, there was a pair of fairy wings waiting for me on the end of the bed. On top of them there was a note:

Love, the fairy boy.

I held them close to my face; the pink glitter twinkled in the sunlight. I could smell him—smell fire smoke and grass and salt. I inhaled a deep breath of him and closed my eyes.

And I was there: running across the sand, lying under the stars, sitting by the waterfall in the late afternoon sun—my friend and me, surrounded by our very own magic.

Saying goodbye to Shuna was harder than I would have thought it could be on the first day she walked into my bedroom at the beginning of summer. That felt like a lifetime ago. I no longer knew who that boy was; the boy hiding in the shadows under the duvet in darkened rooms. I was ready to come out now. And it wouldn't have happened without her.

'Goodbye, my dear boy,' she said, placing both of her hands on my shoulders. Her eyes were as bright as ever. I didn't know how something so dark could be so brilliantly light at the same time.

'Thank you, Shuna,' Dad said. 'For everything—I honestly can't thank you enough.'

'You're welcome any time, Toby. You know that.'

'Thank you, Shuna,' I said. 'I really mean it.'

'I know you do,' she said. 'I hope these rolling beaches and blue skies have finally shown you what a magical thing this life can be, if you only let it.'

'It has.'

'Don't ever forget,' she said.

I picked up my backpack and followed Dad into the waiting taxi, walking past animal statues and brightly coloured stones.

I looked back at the rebel cottage, the pebbled walls and bright blue roof, and Shuna, standing amongst it all; amongst a festival of colour, the centre of her own universe. 'Never forget,' she shouted, leaning over the wall as the car pulled away from the cottage and moved to the end of the lane.

I knew I never would.

The taxi turned into our street, and the first thing I noticed was how small it was. The houses didn't look real—just brown blocks with windows and doors thrown in. Boxes. Even the flats on the opposite side didn't look the same; the brand new double-glazed windows and shiny white doors were nothing compared to the things I had seen. Metal bridges were no replacement for mountains, and a dirty brown river was nothing compared to the sea. I had grown; changed to adapt to my habitat. My insides were bigger, full of laughter and memories and appreciation for all of those things.

Still, it surprised me that I felt glad to be back.

Inside, the house was dark, just as we'd left it. I ran up the stairs to my bedroom and threw the curtains open.

The backfield looked so tiny, so dirty and downtrodden. I began to laugh. I had obsessed over those other boys, as if they were really something special. But they were just kids, most of them shorter and younger than me—smoking to look more grown up, laughing to hide the things they really felt. There was nothing special about them at all. They were nothing compared to the people I had met.

In a way, I felt sorry for them. People weren't supposed to

live in boxes. There was a whole world beyond the Scotswood Road; a sea at the end of the Tyne, and mountains that looked like giants beyond the valley. People were supposed to see it all, to feel the sun warming the back of their neck or dip their toes in cold seawater and swim and move to the rhythm of the tide.

And closer to home, there was beauty in Newcastle, in the sky and the valley and the old city buildings, all there for the taking.

The gangs on the backfield didn't seem to want to see it. Didn't want to go further than what they knew—a mud-trodden field, or the road along the top of the houses with a chippy at the end of it. Maybe it wasn't the estate that boxed them all in; maybe it was something else, something inside of them. I could definitely relate to that.

But, like a chameleon, I had changed colour to match my surroundings; I was blue sea and yellow sand and the red of a sunrise that came before a storm. I had grown. If I stuck out like a sore thumb before, I definitely would now.

That didn't matter. They didn't bother me anymore. I wasn't like them, and that was fine. I didn't want to be. I was my own person, just as important as anyone else. Their hold over me had smashed into bits.

I wasn't a boy like them. I wasn't a girl. I wasn't even in

the middle. I had put one foot in front of the other and had begun the journey towards being me. I had found that I was actually so far away from them that I may as well have lived on the moon. And I couldn't be happier about that. Because the best people, like the best sunrises, or best stars, or best summer days spent with friends, were unpredictable, wild, and completely unique.

My door opened. Dad appeared with a roll of bin liners in his hand. 'I'm going to clear that garden, if you want to help,' he said. 'It's a state.'

'Alright,' I said.

I followed him down the stairs, into the light.

It really was such a mess. I didn't know how we'd lived with it for so long. The weeds were as tall as my waist, twisting and stretching and spilling over the front wall like green and brown claws, holding empty lager cans, and fags, and plastic bags. I couldn't wait to get rid of it all, to clear it away so that we could line the front wall with brightly coloured holey stones to remind us of Shuna's garden. Or plant grass on the lawn and flowerbeds around it, like the front garden of a proper house—a proper home.

I opened my bag and dived into it all, tearing the rubbish from the clutches of the ground. Some of it was gripped so tightly that my fingers turned pink and red as I wrestled it away.

I made my way to the bottom wall, and there, through the twisted remains of a dead bush, I met a familiar pair of eyes—wide, staring and mischievous as ever.

'Alright,' she said.

'Alright,' I said.

She looked exactly as I remembered her. Everything else may have been different, but I could still see Naseera Connolly, clear as anything.

'You've been gone ages,' she said. 'Me mam said you weren't coming back, but I knew you wouldn't leave without saying bye.' The widest grin spread across her face, and I knew everything was all right again. I knew we were still friends.

I smiled too. 'Course not,' I said.

'You're looking well,' she said. 'So, summer was good then?'

'The best.'

'You still missed me, though?'

'Shut up, Naz,' I said. I had never called her that before.

Dad appeared behind me, his hand placed on my shoulder. 'Are you staying for tea, Naseera?' he said.

'What?' said Naseera, her voice far quieter than I had ever heard before.

'Do you want feeding?' said Dad.

She nodded, slowly at first, but gradually getting faster; gradually understanding the changes that had happened over the summer. 'Aye,' she said.

'Take this,' said Dad, holding out a twenty-pound note. 'Run up to your mam's and get us three rounds of cod and chips. Extra batter.'

'She'll give us loads extra,' she said, reaching out a tiny hand and taking the money. She ran to the end of the street and turned the corner.

Dad slid his hand down my back and rubbed, and we walked up the path together.

Just beside the front step, growing in the grass, I noticed something hidden amongst much taller weeds. It was a dandelion clock. Its head was still completely round and untouched. Un-blown. I reached down and pulled it from the ground, then twisted it between my thumb and forefinger, seeing every tiny seed inside.

I looked at Dad, at his new smiling face. 'What happens after,' I said, 'when you've got what you wished for?'

His smile grew even wider, moving his cheeks up towards his eyes. I could finally see Shuna in him. 'You go home, son,' he said. 'You go home.'

I took in a deep breath and blew, watching each tiny speck

swirl away across the rooftops.

And, as the setting sun turned the chimneys, the bridges, and the houses on the other side of the valley golden, I looked on, knowing that home was exactly where I was.

Acknowledgements

I would like to thank my dad for reading endless drafts and helping me out of so many tight spots, my mam for always supporting me (and always asking questions), and my sister because I don't want you to feel left out! To my grandparents—thank you for telling me stories. With special thanks to all of my friends and family for being so patient with me. Shout-out to Sheila, for the cake and reality checks; Lizzie, for reading everything I send you; and to my copy-editor Karen, for being so efficient and easy to work with.

A massive thank you to my partner Chris, for your kindness and patience when I've been lost somewhere in the depths of my head. Thank you for challenging me and always being so present.

Finally, I would like to thank my fourteen-year-old self for deciding to keep a diary and thus providing the voice of Star. You're going to be fine!

About the Author

Daniel Tawse is from Newcastle, and now lives in South East London. He spent his childhood going on adventures in Northumberland, and his teenage years writing diaries about how much he didn't fit in at school. Daniel moved to London to train at The Arts Educational Schools, and spent his twenties performing in various guises. Now in his thirties, he has gained an MA in History from the University of Northumbria and has started turning his past adventures into stories for a wide audience. He is a passionate advocate for LGBTQI+ rights, and through his work aims to provide authentic LGBTQI+ characters to demonstrate positive and relatable voices for all readers.

Q&A with the Author

What inspired you to write Fairy Boys?

The story is loosely based on my own teenage experiences, so I feel like it's been inside of me for a while. I had written another book and was on the millionth draft when I got some feedback on the manuscript about changing some of the elements in the story. Everything I tried to do just didn't seem to work at all, but through endless trying, a fresh idea pinged into my head, using the central character from that story. I was kind of all out of creative energy at that point, so when something new came along I ran with it. I didn't expect it to turn into a story of its own; my main focus was to make the previous one better, as I had worked on it for a long time and didn't want to let it go. But when I did, the magic started to happen and I really found my voice as a writer. It's actually worked out pretty well for both projects.

What is the other project?

It's the first book in a trilogy called *The Boy From Zoa.* It's set between modern day London and the mythical island of Zoa, where all of the un-chosen creatures of the world have lived since the flood of Noah's Arc. It's a middle-grade adventure story with winged soldiers and dark mermaids and underwater cities. And it, of course, has LGBTQI+ characters, as I think it is so important to normalise LGBTQI+ voices for young readers. Watch this space!

Sounds great! Fairy Boys *has a gender-fluid protagonist—is gender incongruence something you wanted to bring attention to?*

Initially, it wasn't something I thought about. I still use the pronoun 'he' when writing about Star, because of the place he is in his life when the story begins. I didn't plan for Star to be non-binary or fluid; it really didn't occur to me that I should categorise him like that. It was a friend, who had read parts of an early draft, who suggested that Star was non-binary. That was a sort of *eureka* moment for me, and helped me understand Star better. From then on I became obsessed with telling this story, so that young gender-fluid readers, or any readers, could have a relatable protagonist who is flawed and funny and emotional and human, and also just happens to be gender-fluid. Literature for younger readers is definitely starting to include more LGBTQI+ characters, which I think is fantastic, but the danger is to only present these characters as their gender or sexuality. Gender has to be shown in all of its wonderful colours, and it also doesn't have to be a character's main trait. I wanted *Fairy Boys* to project a message to young readers that says 'you don't have to be defined by your gender'.

If I ever wrote another book about Star, it would be a continuation of his journey to finding his authentic self. This is the story of his beginnings. I see him in the future evolving into a beautiful creature, causing havoc in the LGBTQI+ community in Newcastle. Hang on, where's my pen …

Have you always wanted to be a writer, and do you have more stories planned?

I have always been a writer. For as long as I can remember I've made books and scripts and told stories. I didn't think of it as a career path; I suppose I wasn't encouraged to go in that direction—I didn't fit in at school, therefore I didn't do too well academically and I always thought that stories were only told by academics. I feel differently now. I believe everybody has a story to tell, and everybody should be encouraged to tell it. I originally trained as an actor, which is really just another branch of storytelling, but I never really found my feet. Writing feels like a homecoming for me; it feels familiar and secure but also incredibly exciting. I write better than I talk. If I were speaking these answers they wouldn't be half as cohesive! And yes, many more stories exist in me head.

What were your favourite books and authors growing up?

I loved books with strong characters and heart. I loved Judy Bloom and her 'Fudge' stories. I always identified with Sheila Tubman, because she acted in a certain way but her internal monologue was quite different. I was very much like that as a child—and as an adult. Also, I have always loved fairy tales, my favourite being *The Little Mermaid* by Hans Christian Andersen. I feel like folk tales and fairy tales are embedded in the culture of the North East; I think it must have something to do with its close proximity to Scandinavia, the home of the fairy tale. Growing up, stories were always in the air. I still love going home and listening to them.

Lastly, who is your favourite character in Fairy Boys*?*

This one isn't hard for me at all. What can I say—I'm ruthless. It's Kitty. For me, she holds the most mystery out of all of them. Even when I was creating her, I never really got to the bones of what she was about. It was like I wasn't allowed; like she didn't want me to see, which I'm totally fine with—as a writer I think its important that you allow your characters to take on a life of their own.

Kitty is obviously a magical creature, which I love. In my mind she's somewhere between Mae West and Ginger Spice. She has a wild side but she is also instinctively maternal. In my mind, she was always a transwoman because I knew she had faced and overcome real adversity in her life, which gave her a certain kind of strength that is synonymous with the LGBTQI+ community. She’s a tough cookie with a heart of milk chocolate, which is why I adore her.

22282973R00154

Printed in Great Britain
by Amazon